Pre-Columbian Woven Treasures

IN THE NATIONAL MUSEUM OF DENMARK

LENA BJERREGAARD

Pre-Columbian Woven Treasures
IN THE NATIONAL MUSEUM OF DENMARK

THE NATIONAL MUSEUM OF DENMARK
UNION ACADÉMIQUE INTERNATIONALE

Pre-Columbian Woven Treasures

IN THE NATIONAL MUSEUM OF DENMARK

© Lena Bjerregaard

Editor: *Inge Schjellerup, Corpus Antiquitatum Americanensium*
Graphic design and production: *Freddy Pedersen*
Photos: *Torben Huss*

All drawings by author, except otherwise mentioned

Printed in Denmark 2002

ISBN 87-89384-91-1

We would like to express our gratitude to

*Her Majesty Queen Margrethe II and Prince Henrik's
Archaeological Foundation,*

Lademanns Fond,

Tips- og Lottomidlerne,

Davids Samling

Lilian og Dan Finks Fond

which made this publication possible.

CONTENTS

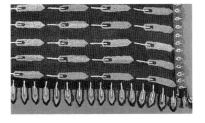

INTRODUCTION

The collection of pre-Columbian Peruvian textiles in the Danish National Museum consists of around 500 items, which were all found in graves. The textiles are mainly garments that were used for wrapping the mummies. The mummies were buried in subterranean burial chambers in the sandy desert on the central and southern coast of Peru, from where they were excavated around AD 1900. The burials originate from about 500 BC to AD1550 and are dated by their style, material, and technology.

The pre-Columbian Peruvians mastered all the textile technologies which were known in Europe before the industrialisation – and even a few more e.g. discontinuous warp, double wrap and possibly some of the supplementary warp and weft techniques (d'Harcourt 1975). Most of these techniques are represented in this collection – although unfortunately ikat and some open-works are missing.

The textiles were excavated in the late nineteenth and early twentieth century, by archaeologists who documented their work, by amateurs and by grave robbers.

Most of the textiles in the National Museum were excavated in Pachacamac. Pachacamac was a ceremonial temple site south of Lima and served as an immense burial ground from the beginning of this era until the Spanish conquest in 1532. In fact many of the encountered textiles are not local, but imported from other cultures, or they are made in Pachacamac, not in the local style but in the style of the ruling culture (provincial Inca for instance) for the local nobility or the representatives of the occupying power.

The other textiles in the collection are from Paracas (southern Peru, 500 BC - AD 500) or Inca textiles from the Peruvian highlands from 1450-1550.

When there is a difference in the provenience between the statements in the archives of the National Museum and in the obvious manufacturing cultures, the names of these cultures are mentioned in brackets after the provenience. The estimation of a textile's age is documented by the related culture.

The textile collection was established at the National Museum between 1882 and 1988; the major part was acquired between 1920 and 1930.

The earliest incoming textiles have O.D.I.c numbers. Some of them are from the Danish Galathea Expedition that circumnavigated the globe in 1845-47. These textiles entered the Museum in 1882.

The museum numbers between O.4030 and O.4377 all belong to the Gretzer collection and were acquired by the museum from the Königliches Museum für Völkerkunde (Today: Ethnologisches Museum) in Berlin in 1922-23. They were either bought from grave robbers or excavated by W. Gretzer. Gretzer was a German businessman who lived in Peru from 1871-1904 and worked as an amateur archaeologist in the late 1890s. After his return to Germany he sold his huge collection of textiles and pottery to museums in Germany.

The textiles with CN numbers belong to the collection of Christiani and Nielsen – a

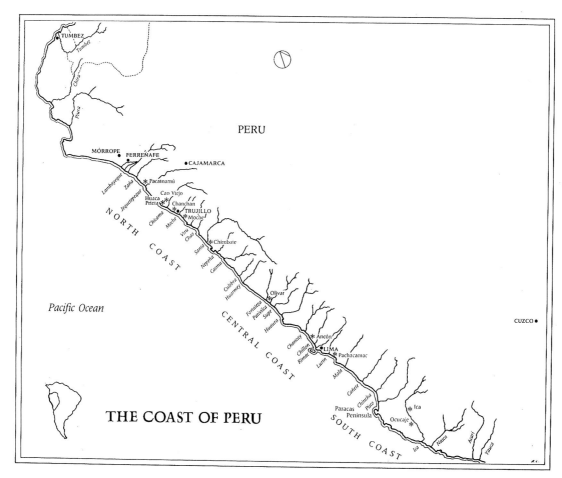

ill. 1. The coast of Peru. (Engelstad, 1985)

Danish engineering firm with agencies all over the world and a firm in Peru around 1950. They were donated to the National Museum in 1988. The remaining pieces are from different private collections.

Most of the textiles in the National Museum are fragments – either due to the fact that grave robbers deliberately cut the textiles off the mummies in their search for gold, or they cut the textiles in smaller pieces in order to sell the fragments (as has happened to Coptic textiles, where usually all the plain weave was cut out leaving only the tapestry). There is also evidence that even European museum staff members cut away pieces, in order to trade with other museums (O.4288 c) or that collectors cut off fragments to send to their friends, as a "souvenir of a pleasant afternoon" (O.6999). However, the museum has several complete pieces.

THE STATE OF PRESERVATION

The original preservation conditions, in an almost sterile environment in the dry desert sand, "one of the driest deserts known" (Engelstad 1985) has been optimal for the textiles. Degradation of organic material needs either oxygen or light and/or humidity. As both light and humidity have been absent during centuries, where the mummies were buried, the textiles were remarkably well preserved at the time of their excavation. Most of the brightly coloured yarns have also maintained their vivid colours.

How and where the textiles were stored, until they reached the National Museum of Denmark, is only known for few of the textiles. In the museum and in the private collections we know of, they were stored in various ways. The O.D.I.c numbered textiles arrived at the National Museum, after a long journey by sea and were stored for some years in the Danish Museum of Decorative Art in Copenhagen as well as in other museums and institutions. In the beginning they were stored unmounted in the Danish Museum of Decorative Art and after some time they were mounted on cardboard. Some of the textiles from the Gretzer collection were exhibited in the National Museum of Denmark, sewn onto a piece of brown cotton cloth and mounted on cardboard, framed behind glass. They remained on exhibition in the museum from the 1930s until 1974 (Engelstad 1985). The colour of the background material faded over the years, but the textiles themselves did not fade very much, which provide proof of the outstanding dyeing methods of the ancient Peruvians compared to the dyeing techniques used by the museum staff in Copenhagen in the 1930s. The remaining part of the Gretzer textiles have been kept in storage, many of them sewn onto a piece of cotton cloth and mounted between two heavy pieces of cardboard.

For approximately 15 years, the Christiani & Nielsen textiles were on exhibition in glass show cases in the entrance hall of the firm's Danish office. A photograph in the agency's newsletter from 1972 shows the hall full of bright daylight.

It remains unknown in which way the remaining textiles that came to the museum from various private collections were stored after their excavation. They have not been on exhibit in the National Museum of Denmark.

Compared to European textiles found in burials in bogs, sarcophagus or in earth graves, the Peruvian textiles seem to be in a very good condition. In general, they have maintained their vivid colours throughout the many centuries of being buried, the decades of storage and/or exhibition in private collections or museums. The state of brittleness of the textiles differs. In this analysis the textiles have been numbered from 1 to 5 according to their state of preservation (no.5 being the most brittle). This system of numbering was created by subjective surface analysis based on: grip, fibre loss and microscopy.

THE HISTORY OF PERUVIAN TEXTILES

In 1532 the Spanish conquistador Francisco Pizarro conquered Peru. At that time the Incas ruled over all Peru, Ecuador, Bolivia and part of Chile. But at the time of the Spanish conquest, the Inca reign and influence had lasted about 100 years only. The Inca civilisation was the last culture based on cultural traditions and highly developed earlier cultures that had been rising and falling through thousands of years on the western side of the South American continent.

The earliest textiles surviving in South America are from the Guitarrero Cave in Callejón de Huaylas in Peru where levels dated to 8.600-8.000 BC contain examples of spiral interlocking and open simple twining, with a Z weft from the pre-ceramic period (Olsen Bruhns 1994). Complicated twined and patterned fibres are from around 2.500 BC at Huaca Prieta on the north coast (Bird and Hyslop 1985), cotton textiles from 2.200 BC at La Galgada (Burger 1992) and by 1.000 BC weaving was established in the Chavin culture.

THE PARACAS TEXTILES

The oldest Peruvian textiles in the National Museum of Denmark are fragments of embroidered mantles from the Paracas culture, which flourished on the south coast of Peru in the last centuries BC. By then large political units, urban centres and sophisticated economic systems involving commercial trade on a regular basis over large distances had developed in the central Andean region. The major deity of the Paracas culture was the Oculate Being, who was associated with knives and trophy heads. This is the first evidence of the widespread warfare and head taking, which characterized the centuries to come (Olsen Bruhns 1994).

The Paracas textiles are made of both wool and cotton and manufactured in very intricate techniques and demonstrate an enormous variety of colours. Especially the techniques of discontinuous warp and weft weaving, loop stitch embroidery without foundation cloth, and stem stitch embroidery must be mentioned as the highlights of these people's craft.

Paracas textiles were first found at the beginning of the 1920's. In 1926 the Peruvian archaeologist Julio C. Tello initiated his investigations at the Paracas peninsula. During

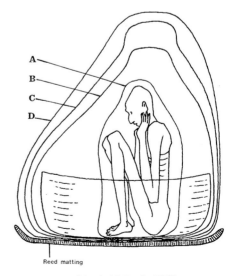

ill. 2. The wrapping layers of the fardel (Paul, 1979).

the next two years he excavated 429 conical shaped mummy bundles, some of them including more than one hundred textiles. A larger mummy bundle is around 150 cm high and has a diameter at the bottom of 150 cm. It could consist of: the body wrapped in a deer skin and placed in a funerary basket, with fifteen woven bands and various pieces of clothing, tucked in around the body, which was then wrapped in twenty-five plain woven fabrics (some of them more than 10 m long), sixteen embroidered mantels, five ponchos, five turbans, a feathered tunic and a headband (Paul 1979).

All the excavated mummies were male elite inhabitants of Paracas. They had deformed sculls. Some of their garments came in sets; a skirt and a mantle with the same embroidered pattern. The iconography in the decorations point towards garments for rituals, or they might indicate the social status of the owner. Some of the garments seem to have been used by the deceased person when he was alive, but others are completely new, and could be gifts given either before or after death. Some of the bundles contain unfinished textiles, but whether they were grave offerings, or just left unfinished, when the person died, has not been established (Paul 1979).

The mummy bundles were transported to the Anthropological Museum in Lima. In 1930 Julio C. Tello resigned the directorship of the museum for political reasons and the burial grounds of Paracas were left open for the grave robbers to explore (Bird and Hyslop 1985). From this period plenty of Paracas textiles started to arrive in European and American Museums (among others the Göteborg collection). Still, most of the Paracas textiles are in the Anthropological museum in Lima where many mummy bundles have not yet been unwrapped (personal experience). Until the 1970s most of the museum´s textiles were kept in wooden boxes in the sometimes flooded basement in the museum in Lima. Since then metal storage

shelves and air conditioning have been installed, which has been an essential improvement especially as the relative humidity in Lima most of the year reaches 98 %.

Later elaborate single graves were found in Paracas, and family graves with people of all ages and presumably of both sexes (Paul 1979).

THE PACHACAMAC TEXTILES

About 350 of the pieces today in the National Museum in Denmark were bought from Ethnologisches Museum in Berlin. They belong to the Gretzer collection and were excavated in Pachacamac on the coast just south of Lima.

According to a myth Pachacamac was the son of the sun, and the creator and protector of man. The place where he threw himself in the sea, supposedly to avoid a family strife, is where his temple and the town bearing his name came to be. The main shrine at Pachacamac had an oracle, which was worshipped and consulted from the beginning of our era up until the Spanish conquest by pilgrims from all over the empire. The main importance of the shrine was from AD 800–1200. One of the Spanish chroniclers Cieza de Leon describes the cult in the 1550s:

Only the chiefs and pilgrims bringing gifts were considered worthy to be buried in the temple vicinity. So the textiles from the burials of Pachacamac must therefore have belonged to people of the upper classes. They were not necessarily produced locally, although similarity to textiles from other centres of the Central Coast suggests that this region was a cultural entity (Engelstad 1984).

According to Max Uhle, a German archaeologist who excavated large areas in Pachacamac around 1900, it was an immense cemetery with an estimated 80.000 graves. There were graves in open cemeteries, under house dwellings and inside the temples. Both men, women and children were buried here. Uhle describes the graves, as follows:

The tombs generally were constructed in a very solid manner, built of stone or adobe in the form of chambers of a conical or cylindrical form; a few were roofed with stones, but the majority had a covering of cane matting or some similar material. The mummies generally have the shape of bales or packages with a false human head attached, the face of which is carved in wood or is merely painted upon a stuffed cushion. The positions were found to be similar in most cases, facing east and towards the temple at the same time (Uhle and Shimada 1991).

Cieza de Leon mentions that most of the graves were looted in earlier times and were still being looted when he visited Peru in the first decade after its discovery:

Many of the graves have been opened and are still explored, for, ever since the Spanish conquest of the empire, much gold and silver were found in this way. (Engelstad 1984).

Jorge de Ulloa, who visited the place in the early eighteenth century, says:

No idea can be formed of the topography of the ancient city and of its houses, as large mounds of adobe cover every part of it, debris of walls pulled down in the search for tombs and the treasures supposed to be concealed therein, since wild tales of some earlier finds spurred the people on, to do this. The graves were almost all filled up with sand and adobe, and the ones still remaining are the ones devoid of objects of gold and silver, or containing but few of these (Engelstad 1984).

Not only local textiles were found in Pachacamac but also many imported textiles from the Chimu culture on the northern coast and from the Wari and Inca cultures in the central Andes. Some of the Inca style textiles, though, were probably woven locally and are thus termed *Provincial Inca* (Rowe 1992).

Around the year 1470 the Incas conquered the entire Peruvian coast. They were eminent administrators who sent ambassadors from their capital Cuzco in the mountains to all the new provinces to govern and collect the state products. As writing did not exist in pre-Columbian Peru the first information we

ill.3. Spinning and weaving procedures in 1500-1600 Peru. Guaman Poma de Ayala (Paris 1936)

received in Europe on ancient Peruvian cultures originated from the Incas, i.e. from what the Spanish missionaries or the chroniclers wrote down and later from scientific archaeological excavations. The Incas used their *quipus* for counting and a sort of symbolic message system *tocapu*, which was woven into their tunics and their belts. The understanding of these pictographs were probably only known by the high Inca nobility, and has not yet been deciphered by today's scientists (Rowe 1992).

One of the most important sources of information comes from the commented picture-book, written by Guaman Poma de Ayala, an Indian from a noble family. This document from the end of the 16th century was rediscovered in The Royal Library, Copenhagen in 1912 (reprint Paris 1936). Guaman Poma de Ayala explains many things about the Inca society and among others about the textile production.

Two kinds of textiles were woven during Inca times: the *awasqa* and the *qompi*. The *awasqa* was a coarser weaving, woven on the backstrap loom, and the *qompi* a tapestry weaving made on an upright loom. The *qompi* was the finest kind of tapestry woven by the *acllas* (the virgins of the sun), the second best were made by the wives of the province government officials and the third category was woven by specially educated male weavers who wove in order to pay the provincial taxes to the Inca. All *qompies* belonged to the Inca and nobody outside of the royal family were allowed to wear them, except when given as a present from the ruler. But then, *qompies* seem to have been the most common gift from the ruler to his subjects, used as payment for a service or as a bribe.

The patterns in the *qompi* tunics were standardised, but woven in many different colours (Rowe 1978).

None of the original Inca textiles existing today are from after 1550. By then, the Spanish system had destroyed the Inca cultural traditions and the Catholic Church had eliminated the ancient burial rituals.

GARMENTS

During the reign of the Incas, a person's clothing showed the social status of the individual and his province of origin. For instance, there existed a type of headband, the *llaut'u*, made of braided cords, which was worn by the inhabitants of Condesuyu. The *llaut'u* worn by the Inca himself was of crimson and blue colours, wound around the head in four or five coils, with a fringe *masqua paicha* in the same colours, covering the forehead. The heir of the Inca wore the same ornament, except that the *masqua paicha* was yellow. The nearest relatives wore the *llaut'u* with two red and yellow tassels on the right temple instead of the fringe. The *llaut'us* of the nobles were black (Shimada 1991). Presumably the previous cultures of Peru had a more or less similar system of marks of social status and identification.

The garments of ancient Peru were not cut and tailored. They were all manufactured in the desired measurements and maybe sewn together. Cutting a textile was very seldom (Murra 1958). The only cut textiles in this

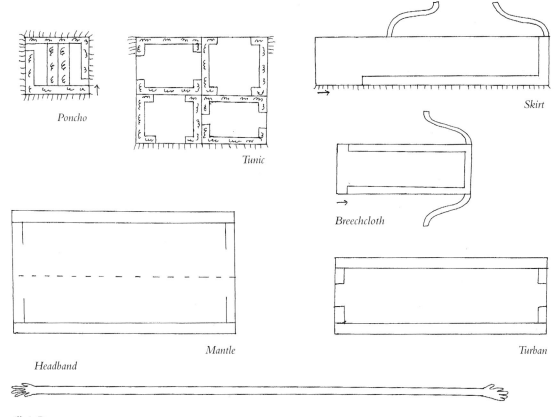

Poncho

Tunic

Skirt

Breechcloth

Mantle

Turban

Headband

ill. 4. *Paracas garments*

collection are tapestry patches that were to be sewn onto the tunics from the late Pachacamac period (1200-1400). They were woven in bands and then cut and sewn onto the thin gauze like cotton fabric.

Most garments were rectangular and wrapped around the body.

In the Paracas culture the following pieces of men's clothing were used (Paul 1979):

• a breechcloth with a belt for tying, approximately 1.00 x 0.50 m. The breechcloth was pulled between the legs, with the free end secured by the ties, which was wrapped around the waist. The flap hung down to the back of the wearer. The breechcloth was ornamented along the long sides and the top.
• a wrap around skirt (approximately 2.50 x 0.50 m) with two ties attached to the upper long edge. Tassels or fringes are found at the bottom, and a decorated edge along the bottom and the side.
• a poncho which is a small shoulder covering rectangular textile with a neck slit and not sewn along the sides. Often it has fringes around the edges.
• a tunic which is bigger than the poncho and sewn along the sides, often with sleeves like fringes.
• a turban of a gauze like material approximately 1.90 x 0.80 m.
• a headband approximately 6 cm wide and up to 9 m long, often ending in a hand with 5 fingers.
• a mantle approximately 2.75 x 1.30 m normally sewn together lengthwise from two pieces.

The most outstanding of the Paracas textiles are plain woven fabrics with stem stitch embroidery (O.6999 a, b, c) and loop stitch figures (H. 6345 and U.N.1). But also discontinuous warp weaving, tapestry, gauze, painted, braided, spranged or looped textiles were produced at the time (for definition of techniques see chapter 6, Technical analyses).

The Pachacamac textiles are largely the same types as the above mentioned, although their dimensions and techniques differ (Montell 1929).

The tunics are all short (about waist length) and wide. Later – after the Wari empire's decline (about 1100 AD) wool got scarcer on the coast, and large thin cotton

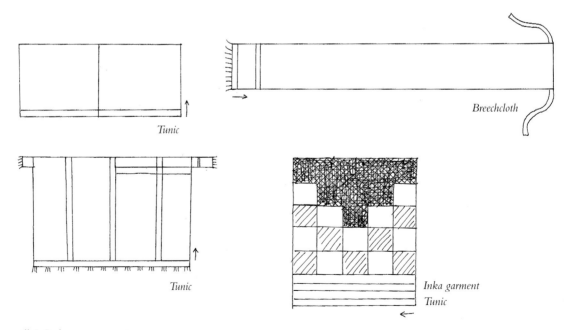

Tunic

Breechcloth

Tunic

Inka garment
Tunic

ill.5. *Pachacamac garments.*

LACVARTA COIA
CHIMBOMAMA
IACHIVRMA

EL DECIMOINGA
TOPAINGA·IV
PANQVI

Reyno hasta charca

chinbo

Reyno tarma dji ta atapillo ni ros bunec huayllac

chayrocha uaro chiri can ya ihas chistap conchoco uaxan ga uuno to allaucaychoca ua

ropa

ill.6. Male and female Inca noble dress. Guaman Poma de Ayala (Paris 1936)

tunics with appliquéd wool/cotton bands and squares with small and narrow sleeves for the wrists became in fashion. (The wool came from the highland, and when the Wari Empire collapsed, the trade between the highlands and the coast became more difficult). The breechcloths are much longer (up to 2 m) and the end flap, opposite the belt is heavily ornamented. It often ends in a fringe.

The preferred techniques were slit tapestry, and later brocade, gauze, and double weave; however all the former techniques were still used. Embroidery though, was no longer used for covering whole pieces of fabric, as in the Paracas culture, and loop-and stem stitching was limited to edging the textiles. The patterns were animals, ritual and mythological beings like in the Paracas days.

In the Inca period (Bosqued and Gomez 1980) the decors of a surrealistic world of gods and mythical beings, which were so widely used in previous cultures, were substituted by ornamental patterns. The tunics became narrower and longer. The centre of the Inca Empire was in the highlands where wool was abundant. Their tunics were woven in interlocked tapestry. They were much heavier than the coastal textiles, as they were made out of wool for both warp and weft, and the weft was very tightly packed (up to about 100 wefts per cm). Also complementary warp patterned textiles in pure wool were favoured by the Incas.

From Guaman Poma de Ayala and from ceramics we know how both men and women were dressed. Men wore breechcloths, tunics, ponchos, headbands and mantels and women wore long tunics, some sewn at the sides, some held together by a belt. Women also had a folded mantle around the shoulders attached by a pin in the front (C.N.6)

Most of the Pachacamac textiles in the collection of the National Museum of Denmark are manufactured locally from locally grown cotton and to a lesser degree from camelid wool, imported from the Andes. However, a few of them are imported (O.4295, O.4294c, O.4294a, O.4333). According to Ann Rowe (1984) these are probably Chimu (North coast of Peru, 1100- 1450 AD) as this is one of the few places in Peru, where weavings with paired warps and single wefts, with even thread count for warp and weft (the paired warps counted for one) and single ply S spun cotton yarns were produced.

Also the tapestries of pure wool were probably imported from the Andean highlands or manufactured locally, but in Inca style (provincial Inca). This applies to O.4331, which in the design shows a resemblance to the late Wari culture (AD 1100 - 1450) but the textiles have an obvious Inca influence (O.4217). The O.4399 is Inca characterised by the Inca pattern and the shape of the tunic (longer that wide), which is strictly Inca.

TABLE OF PRE-COLUMBIAN CULTURES IN PERU:

1532 AD	Spanish conquest
1450	Inca
	Chimu
	Chancay
	Lambayeque
800	Wari
	Moche
500	Nazca
	Paracas
BC 1000	Chavin

FIBRE MATERIAL

COTTON

The Peruvian cotton *(Gossypium barbadense)* is a very resistant kind of short fibred cotton (2,5-5 cm), which occurs naturally in different colours: white, tan, light brown, dark brown and a greyish mauve colour. The cotton fibres are easily removed from the seeds by hand. In pre-Columbian times as well as today the fibres are spun on a spindle without a weight (Majory 1984).

D'Harcourt mentions: "The fineness of the single Peruvian cotton yarns is fine, although not as fine as the delicate muslins woven in ancient times of India"(d'Harcourt 1975).

WOOL

The Peruvian wool comes from the camelids, i.e. vicuña, alpaca, guanaco or lama. The alpaca is most important for textile production, having very long lustrous hair 15-20 cm long and with a thickness of 10-75µm, most of them being around 26µm (Paul 1979). The habitat of the alpaca is between 3.000 and 5.000 m above sea level and the animal is easily domesticated. The vicuña has shorter and finer hair (5-6 cm long and 6-35µm wide fibres). It only inhabits regions above 5.000 m and is not possible to domesticate.

In former times it was killed to obtain the wool. Each vicuña gives ca. 400 g of wool (Majory 1986). During the Inca civilisation it was naturally reserved for the finest textiles for the Incas. The lama was mostly domesticated as a pack animal, its fibres mainly being very coarse (10 -150µm but with a majority of coarser fibres). The guanaco is not a domesticated animal and has very fine wool, but it is rare (today it only lives in Patagonia). The guanaco is supposed to be the ancestor of the lama and the alpaca; the vicuña is a different branch of the family (Wildman 1954).

The scale pattern of the wool of the camelids has an irregular waved mosaic structure. The fibre scales of the camelids do not stand out from the fibre, as the sheep fibre scales, which make them appear much smoother than the sheep's wool fibres, and for the same reason they are very hard to felt.

Medulla is only present in the coarsest fibres, and can be either continuous or fractional. The cross-section of the larger camelid medullas may have a very characteristic 3-4 channelled amoeba-like shape. The non dyed naturally dark fibres may have a clear rind (Wildman 1954).

The 2-ply woollen yarns of ancient Peru yield some of the very finest hand spun wool in the world according to d'Harcourt (1975).

TOOLS

All Pre-Columbian textiles were made from hand spun yarns. A loose hanging spindle with a weight was used to spin the wool. Cards to comb the wool have not been found in the Andes. Today in the Potosi area of Bolivia, the Indians do not cut the wool from their sheep, but skin the sheep, pluck tufts of hair, and spin them immediately in order to avoid the hair getting tangled up. But according to d'Harcourt (1975) only the wild and very shy vicuña were killed in pre-Columbian times in order to use its wool, the other camelids' fleece was cut off and spun. Some of the finest woollen yarns were spun in Peru before the conquest and its uniformity of size and quality in the Inca period would hint at the existence of spinning centres, from where the yarns were exported to the rest of the Empire (d'Harcourt 1975).

The cotton was spun on spindles without whorls, probably by holding the spindle almost horizontal and resting it in a calabash bowl – like today. Seeds of the American cotton *(Gossypium barbadense)* are easily removed from the fibres. The removing of seeds and the spinning were probably always done in one process, as they are today (personal experience).

LOOMS

Two different looms were used in Peru before the conquest, the horizontal and the vertical loom (Stone-Miller 1992).

The horizontal loom was stretched with a belt between the weaver and a fixed point usually higher up, so the loom would have a sloping angle being lowest nearest to the weaver. This is the back-strap loom. The weaver, bending forward and stretching backward, regulated the tension of the loom. The weaving was strung on to a top- and a bottom-beam by means of a strong cotton cord, which would be removed after the weaving was completed, and leave a selvage at top and bottom of the weaving. The weaving would by means of thin needles be woven all the way through, so the textile finally would have four selvages.

The warp may be as long as desired on this kind of loom, as it is rolled up on an extra bottom beam while the weaving progresses. The weaving can only be up to about 75 cm wide, as the weaver has to be able to control the whole width of the fabric beating the weft down with a heavy weaving sword.

The loom could also be horizontally stretched on 4 corner stones and held in place by 4 small poles or nails, as the loom used all over the Andes today. It has the same advantages and limitations as the back-strap loom. The commoners would only use this kind of loom.

The upright loom was developed during the Wari Empire and taken over by the Incas. During the Inca Empire, only the finest weavings, *qompi*, made by the most selected and skilled weavers were woven on this kind of loom.

The warp is vertically stretched on a horizontal beam resting on two upright poles. A bottom beam is placed at the other end of the warp. The weaving starts from the bottom and proceeds upwards. This loom could be set up in any desired width up to 2-3 m; Stone-Miller (1992) suggests that some looms could be folded after weaving the first half, so the weaver could stay sitting on the ground weaving all way through the textile, but maybe, she could just stand up for the second half (these pre-conquest textiles were in length, never too long to be reached by a standing person – they were all meant for clothing, the length being for instance the width of a tunic). Some of the Inca weavings (C.N.0) are woven with the reverse surface changing side during the weaving; on this loom the weaver could go round to the back of the loom and proceed weaving from here when required. The large Inca and Wari tunics are woven on this kind of loom being about 2 m wide and 1 m long. The tunics were woven from the side, so that the warp direction was horizontal when worn. Only woollen textiles in tapestry weaving were woven on this type of loom.

The beams of the loom, the shed sticks and the weaving sword were made of strong wood; especially the weaving sword had to be of a heavy sort of wood. For laying in the patterns a lama-bone was used, as is still the case in the region.

Needles for sewing and embroidering were made of cactus thorns or metal (gold, silver or copper).

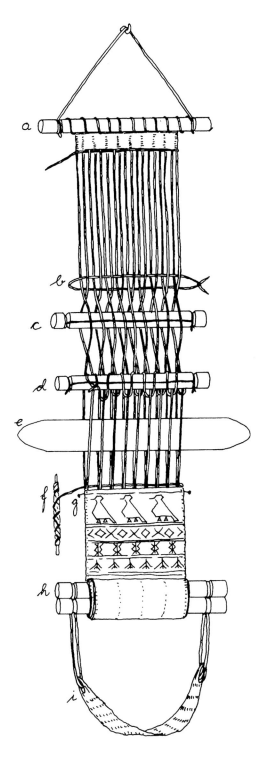

ill. 7. The Backstrap loom:
a: Top beam
b: Cross-tie
c: Rod
d: Heddle
e: Batten
f: Shuttle
g: Stretcher
h: Bottom beam.

(Bjerregaard, 1977)

TECHNICAL ANALYSES

The textile definitions in the following are according to Irene Emery's "The Primary Structures of Fabrics" (1966). The techniques are divided after number of thread elements, and according to weaving and after-weaving techniques presented at random.

The textiles are divided into the following main groups, and the examples found in the collections of the National Museum of Denmark are given in brackets. On the following page the museum numbers are listed behind the techniques, so each technique can be looked up with an example in the appendix.

1.ONE ELEMENT:
simple looping, loop stitch, square knot with "simili velour", peruke stitch.

2.TWO ELEMENTS:
cord wrapping, flat double wrap.

3.ONE SET OF ELEMENTS:
braiding, sprang, warp plaiting.

4.TWO SETS OF ELEMENTS (WEAVING):
Plain weave 1/1, 2/1, plain weave with warp braiding.
Discontinuous warp
Tapestry (slit tapestry, interlocked tapestry).
Complementary weft or warp weave with substituting colours.
Supplementary weaves:
Brocade: (single faced, 2-faced, double faced, lancé).
Supplementary warp patterning.

Supplementary warp and weft patterning.
Double weave.
Gauze weave (simple, complex).
Tube weave.

5.DECORATION OF FABRICS:
tassels, fringes, loop weave, application, tie dye, paint, print, feather mosaic, embroidery.

ONE ELEMENT

The "one element" technique used in ancient Peru, was all done with free-end threads – as opposed to knitting, where a loop of an unbroken thread forms the linking.

Looping: a doubling of a cord or thread back on itself so as to leave an opening between the parts through which another cord or thread may pass (Engelstad 1985).

SIMPLE LOOPING

What builds up simple looping is known as the buttonhole stitch in sewing and lace-making, in rope work as the half-stitch. Depending on whether the looping is loose or tight the fabric created can have an open net-structure or a crochet-like compact feel.

In the collection of the National Museum of Denmark (O.10.268, O.10.267) the looping was used because of its elasticity to create the top part of coca-bags. It held the bag

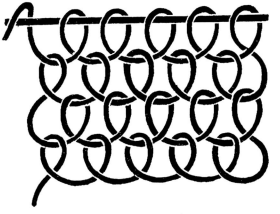

ill.8. Simple looping. (d'Harcourt, 1975)

together. This kind of looping was always made in rather thick cotton yarns.

LOOP-STITCH (OR CROSS-KNIT LOOP):

The loop stitch differs from simple looping in that the loop is taken round the crossing of a loop in the previous row rather than through each loop separately. The loop-stitched fabric completely resembles a fabric made by crossed knitting of the stocking stitch type, but it differs from it in various ways. It is not as elastic as the knitting. It is created from the opposite side from that of the knitting – the rows of knitting made in the order 4 - 3 - 2 - 1 and the loop stitching made in the order 1 - 2 - 3 - 4. In this way the loops in the loop-stitching are closed by the crossing of the yarn, which passes back across itself. Therefore, when pulling the working yarn in loop stitching the loops will not slide and disintegrate one after the other as in true knitting.

The Peruvian loop stitching was used to create little 3-dimentional figures (identical on both sides) which either framed or made up a whole textile or fringes etc. The loop stitching was done around a woven or knotted foundation with the little details looped into the air without foundation. The fibres used were mainly wool.

(H.6345, U.N. 1)

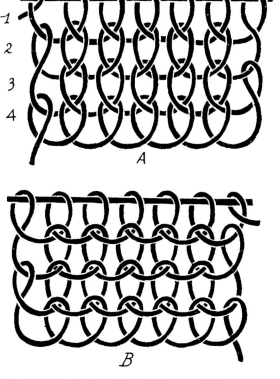

ill.9. Loop stitch-back and front. (d'Harcourt, 1975)

SQUARE KNOT WITH FLOSS "SIMILI VELOUR"

The square knot consists of two half hitches making it a symmetrical, fixed knot. It is known as the Chinese filet knot in the net ground of the filet lace.

In Peru, it was used for various nets and as foundation for the "simili velour" caps, headbands, and furred cords.

In these textiles the foundation cloth consists of a mesh of square knots usually formed with rows of square knots formed either alternately on the right side and the reverse or all on the same side. The square knot netting is usually cotton.

An independent wool yarn is then caught between two consecutive knots forming a loop and the mesh and loop are tightened simultaneously. The woollen pattern loops are either induced in every row of square knots or in every second row. The loops are then cut afterwards.

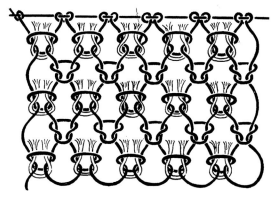

ill. 10. Square knots with simili velour. (d'Harcourt, 1975).

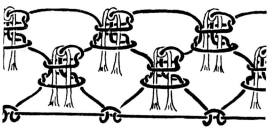

ill. 11. Peruke stich. (d'Harcourt, 1975).

Network with closed loops or cut pile seems to have been used only in the southern region of Peru and only for fine articles like bonnets and headbands; at least no larger specimens are known up to the present. (C.N. 11).

"SIMILI VELOUR" FURRED CORDS

This type of furred cords has a core of cotton yarns. The network which consists of square knots turns in spirals around the cotton core; the knots are all made on the same side – the outer side – and each one contains the cut woollen pile yarn. Thus a tubular article with a "furred" decoration is made.

NETWORK WITH THE PERUKE STITCH

The Peruvians invented another knot for their tight networks: the peruke stitch knot. It is a more complex descendant of the square knot and it is a knot that defies displacement of the independent pile material however slippery it might be. This knotting is commenced by making a knot with the yarn of the network in the form of two half hitches, which lock the yarn of the preceding row of knots and the independent element. But instead of passing directly to the following knot, the yarn of the network forms two loops around the apex of the angle formed

by the independent element. Finally a last loop has to be made and tightening this loop gives the knot the double effect and ties the pile material firmly in the netting. (C.N. 8)

TWO ELEMENTS

CORD WRAPPING

In this technique a number of cotton yarns are serving as a core in the fabric. A spiralling cotton yarn encircled this core. These spiralling yarns were then joined together by a soumak embroidery stitch. Sometimes the embroidery stitches were parallel, sometimes opposed. The latter could resemble chain stitching.

This technique seems to have been possible only by the use of a curved needle (due to the stiffness of the core). According to d'Harcourt archaeological evidence of curved needles actually exists (d'Harcourt 1975).

This technique was used for slings. The core of yarns was in the middle part of the sling stretched flat and woven with a woollen yarn like a weft rep textile. The warp yarns were after the middle part joined together again as core for another encircled and embroidered part. The technique was also used for the top of tassels, or for ornamental borders for certain garments and bags. In some cases the middle core was removed after the embroidery was finished. (O.4032, O.5659, O.10.271

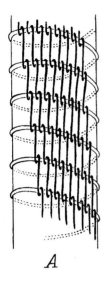
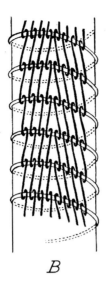
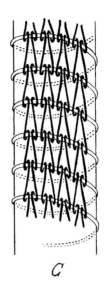

A B C

ill. 12.
Soumack stitches
used in cord
wrapping.
(d'Harcourt, 1975)

FLAT DOUBLE WRAP

The soumak-embroidered cord wrapping technique was also used to create flat double-sided textiles. Coarse cotton yarns are warped on two adjacent, parallel surfaces, as in double cloth weaving. They are joined and covered in stem stitch embroidery by vertical wool yarns, some of which alternate among them selves in passing from one face to the other, as in double weaving. This technique produces a thick and stiff fabric with ornamental motives the same on the two sides, but with reversed colours, as two yarns of different colours are used simultaneously – one on either side of the fabric.

This technique was mainly used for creating decorative hangings under bags, which mostly had a thick woollen fringe attached to them.
(O.4030, O.10.267)

ONE SET OF ELEMENTS

BRAIDING

Braiding is an oblique interlacing where a set of yarns, tied at the top and loose at the bottom are interlocked simply passing over and under each other and changed direction-wise only at the edges of the fabric, where the elements turn back on the opposite diagonal.

The examples in our collection are plain over-one-under-one, comparable to a plain weave textile except for the oblique trend of all elements without differentiation. Theoretically from one to an infinite number of separate yarns can be interlaced in this technique.
(O.D.I.c 204, O.4256)

ill. 13. Braiding.
(d'Harcourt, 1975).

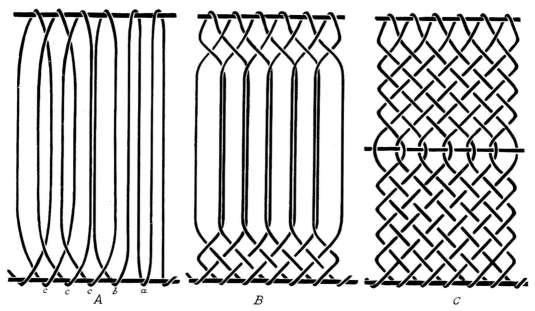

ill. 14. Sprang in the works. The stretched warp system; beginning of the plaiting; securing the finished sprang by a middle thread. (d'Harcourt, 1975)

SPRANG

Sprang is an inter-linking technique done with a warp stretched on a frame. Inter- linking means that the elements consistently link with adjacent or nearly adjacent elements on either side and change their relative positions only slightly through the fabric. The consistent crossings tend to produce an appearance of continuous diagonals across the fabric even though no element moves more than one link to the right or left of its original position.

In sprang the frame stretched warp will link identically at the top and bottom of the frame when the yarns are worked in the middle. When the inter-linking is worked all the way through the warp from the top and bottom to the middle, a securing yarn must be worked through the warp at the middle to hold the two symmetrical halves of the spranged textile, which might otherwise disintegrate.
(O.1031)

WARP PLAITING

Warp plaiting is an open work technique used for ornamental purpose within a woven fabric. After the last weft is inserted in the plain weave, groups of a certain even number of warp threads are separated. Each group is plaited over one under one, either with one or two of the outer warps or with separate wefts over a few passages; then the group is divided into two subsections, each plaited in the same way together with the adjacent subsection of warps on both sides – and so forth. The one warp-plaiting example in the collection of the National Museum of Denmark

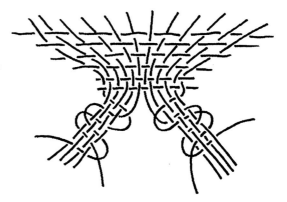

ill. 15. Open works with warp plaiting.

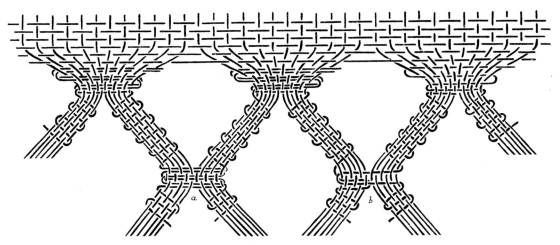

ill. 16. Open works with weft plaiting. (d'Harcourt, 1975).

(O.4136) is plaited with the two outer warps and no wefts, and is therefore grouped under "one set of elements" rather than under weaving, which is made up by "two sets of elements".

This technique can be made also with a weft as active element. It often turns up as a lower border decoration on tunics.

TWO SETS OF ELEMENTS

PLAIN WEAVE

Plain weaving is the simple interlacing of warp threads stretched between two end bars and a weft interlocked from side to side. Each weft unit passes alternately over and under successive warp units, and each reverses the procedure of the one before it i.e. the warps are separated into only two groups, and all warps that lie above one passage of weft lie below the next and continuously. It is possible to vary the expression of the plain weave by spacing the warps and weft differently or by grouping the elements into units – but basically the obverse and the reverse of plain weave are structurally identical.

Some of the most used plain weaves in ancient Peruvian textiles are:

Balanced plain weave (where the warp and the weft counts are completely or almost

identical). O.D.I.c 267, O.4294a, O.6712, O.6790, O.6789, O.4202, O.6999, O.4141, O.4137, O.4138, O.4139

Unbalanced plain weaving, where warp and weft counts differentiate are seen in: O.4131, O.4136, O.4349, O.5674, O.3032, O.4151.

Warp faced plain weaving – where the warps completely cover the wefts, O.D.I.c 236 a, O.4195, O.4374, O.3037, O.4352, O.4294 c, O.4299.

Weft faced plain weaving, where the wefts completely cover the warps (all tapestries). (O.4174, O.4217, O.4277, O.4284)
Plain weave with paired warps or paired wefts or both (O.D.I.c 236 a 2/1, O.4328b 2/2, O.4142 2/2, O.4295, O.4294a, O.6712 2/1, O.4340 2/1)

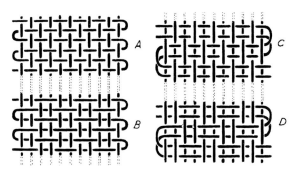

ill. 17. Plain weave. One weft, one warp. One weft, two warps. Two wefts, two warps. (d'Harcourt, 1975).

DISCONTINUOUS WARP

This technique may be the most interesting of the ancient Peruvian techniques. It was probably never used extensively – if at all – outside of Latin America. The technique is a special system of warp construction on which various weaving techniques can be used.

According to a desired pattern the construction consists of various warp segments of different colours, so that the warps, and sometimes also the wefts, turn back at the areas of colour change. To set up an interrupted warp like this, additional scaffold threads or rods are horizontally secured over the warp, and the warp threads reverse around these in the setting up. Sometimes the scaffold threads are left in the finished fabric, sometimes the warps are interlocked to each other, and sometimes the scaffold threads are removed after the weaving is finished and the warps are either held together with a common weft or are sewn together.

The vertical joining of different colour parts can likewise also be either interlocked or left open as slits. Both horizontal and vertical slits would be sewn together after the weaving – actually many of the weavings were woven in narrow bands sewn together afterwards. Renate Strelow, (personal commu-

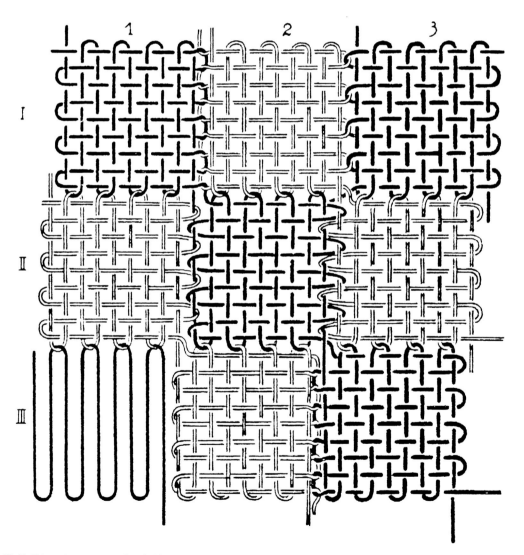

ill. 18. Discontinous warp and weft. (d'Harcourt, 1975).

nication 1998) even suggests that the woven parts as squares or the like, were perhaps all taken apart, dyed and then sewn back together again!

The weavings with discontinuous warps have the unique character of being thin, lightweight fabrics with figurative patterns and solid colours when woven with fine cotton threads in plain weave, an effect that cannot be achieved in any other weaving technique. The technique is also used for heavy warp rep textiles where it gives a softer, more flexible textile than a tapestry woven textile.

The discontinuous warp technique can produce square, as well as slanted or even curved patterns. The pattern units can be extremely small – the Ethnographic Museum, Dahlem, in Berlin has a checked textile with squares between 1,3 and 1,6 cm. Naturally these textiles could not be regularly woven, as there was no room for sheds, but the weft actually must have been sewn into the warp with a needle.
(O.4170, O.4288c, O.4333b, O. 4339, O.1027)

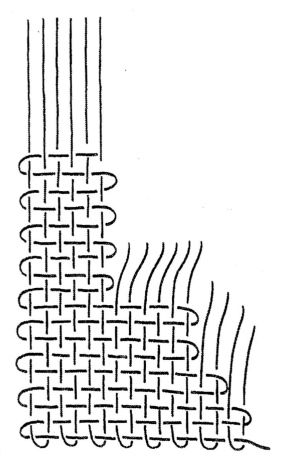

ill. 19. Shaped warp.

SHAPED WARP

This is a technique, where the warp is set up uninterrupted in its full length and then after weaving, the warp is cut and sewn down into the woven fabric. The technique is used both to create slanted shaped textiles (e.g. for the decorative back piece of breechcloths) and for the stepped corner decorations of tunics. The cut warp-threads are sewn into the woven fabric to secure them.
(O.4325c).

TAPESTRY

Tapestry is the name of a patterning with discontinuous wefts in a weft-faced weave. Generally, tapestry involves two fundamental principles: hiding the warp with closely packed wefts to secure solid colour, and weaving independently wefts back and forth each in its own pattern area. The wefts are interlocked only partly across the warp and others are successively substituted to fill out the row, and in this way the wefts create solid colour areas, similar on both sides.

Where the discontinuous wefts meet they can be dovetailed, interlocked or left with open slits.

Dovetailed means that the two meeting wefts turn around the same warp.

Interlocked means that the two meeting

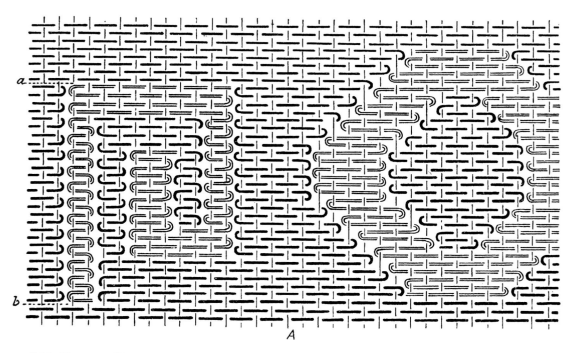

ill.20. Slit tapestry. (d'Harcourt, 1975).

wefts are looped into each other between the warps.

Both dovetailing and interlocking can be done in many different ways, i.e. with each weft, every second or in pairs.

Slit tapestry means that the two meeting wefts turn around neighbouring warps, thus creating an open slit along the vertical pattern lines. These slits can either be left open or sewn together after the weaving is done. Sometimes they are secured every one or two cm by a single interlocked weft.

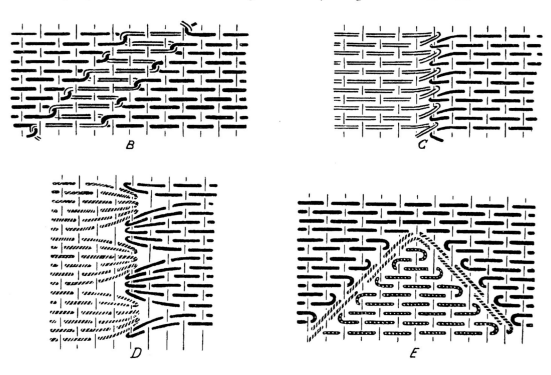

ill.21. Different kinds of dovetailed and interlocked tapestry. (d'Harcourt, 1975).

The two faces of tapestry in woven fabrics are identical in both structure and colour patterning. In Peruvian tapestries all weft ends are concealed in the warp, and no loose ends are left hanging on either side of the weaving.

(Slit tapestry: O.4325c, O.4174, O.4281, O.4311a, O.4311 b, O.4277b, O.4277c, O.4251, O.4243, O.4231, O.4237, O.4325b, O.4407b, O.4366c. Dovetailed tapestry: O. 4331b, O.4217, C.N. 0)

COMPLEMENTARY WEFT WEAVE WITH SUBSTITUTING COLOURS

A special type of tapestry weaving is the complementary weft weaving with substituting colours. In this weaving every second shed has a weft of the same colour – red for instance, as a kind of ground weft. Every other shed has another colour or maybe different colours with discontinuous wefts, as pattern weft. The ground weft always goes over one and under three, front and back. The pattern weft likewise goes under one, over three, but as there are sometimes several colours in a row the wefts may float from one pattern unit to the next, and thus create a textile with a different front and back.

(C.N.0, O.4151, O.4188b, O.4355, O.4238).

SUPPLEMENTARY WEFT WEAVE (BROCADE)

A brocade weaving consists of a simple ground-weave, on top of which extra pattern wefts are inlaid. The ways in which the extra wefts can be interlaced in the weaving are not subject to any consistently applicable limitation, and thus the ways of patterning are almost infinitely varied.

In Peru a plain ground weave or a gauze weave serves as foundation for a brocade patterning. The brocading can be listed as follows:

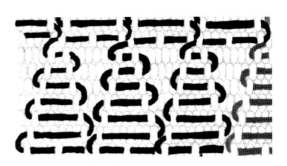

ill.22. Single face brocade.

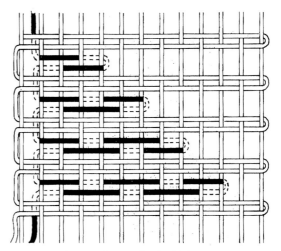

ill.23. Two face brocade. (Engelstad, 1985).

Discontinuous wefts:
- single-faced
- two-faced
- double-faced

Continuous wefts (lancé)
- single-faced
- two-faced
- double-faced

As in tapestry weft-ends are never left hanging loose from a woven fabric, but are always secured between the two warp layers.

In the *single-faced discontinuous weft brocade* the pattern wefts are laid in between the two warp layers and pulled forward on the front side of the weaving, covering a varied number of warp threads. During the weaving the pattern wefts are always hanging to the front side of the weaving. On the backside the pattern wefts never show up.
(O.4299, O.4298).

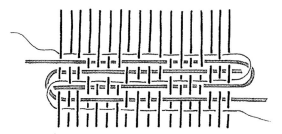

ill.24. Double face brocade.

In the *two-faced discontinuous weft brocade* the pattern wefts are worked through both warp layers. The warp threads covered by the pattern wefts on the front are uncovered on the back and vice versa, and so the negative pattern shows up on the backside of the weaving. During the work, the pattern wefts are always kept on the backside of the weaving. (O.4151).

In the *double-faced discontinuous weft brocade* the pattern weft is worked through both warp layers like in two-faced brocade. But here it is always worked over and under the same number of warp threads (normally 2 or 4 at a time). Without changing the shed the pattern weft is then worked back through the warp in the same way, this time going over all the warp groups it went under at first. In this way the warp threads are covered on both sides with the pattern weft. Only after the pattern weft has been woven back and forth, the sheds are changed and the ground weft is woven.
(O.5674, O.4399).

The lancé brocading variations are the same as the above mentioned. The difference is that the pattern weft, instead of being discontinuous and partial, floats unbroken from selvage to selvage; partly between and partly over the two warp layers.
(O.4340a, O.3032).

WARP REP PATTERNING AND
COMPLEMENTARY WARP

In this technique the warp completely covers the weft. For making stripes across the warp

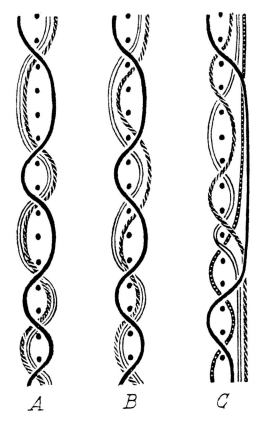

ill.25. Supplementary warp weaves.
(d'Harcourt, 1975).

(along the weft) the warp is in 2 alternate colours and is set up with warps tied together at either end of the loom, so that each colour makes up 2 warp rounds. Typically, the weaving starts with a plain weave creating horizontal stripes on the fabric, as each shed is of a different colour. Then to create a pattern, the warps float over one or three wefts, and thus a pattern will be reversed on the backside (complementary warp). The textiles in this technique can of course have many colours set up in stripes, but each stripe has only 2 alternating colours.
(C.N. 10, O.4216, C.N. 12, O.4301a).

SUPPLEMENTARY WARP

The supplementary warp technique can be set up in 3 or 4 differently coloured yarns. The basic weaving is like warp rep patterning, but on top of that one or two supplementary warps are inserted. Normally, the yarn of the colour that was supposed to be dominant was left floating over 3 wefts, whereas the warp threads on either side were woven in each shed. In that way they were hidden underneath the dominant floating warp threads.
(O.4193).

The two differently coloured warps following the same shed in these weavings could also be left floating on the backside of the textile. An example of this is a cylinder-shaped weaving, where the back-floats are concealed inside the cylinder.
(O.4223).

SUPPLEMENTARY WARP AND WEFT

It is also possible to make a textile with both supplementary warp and supplementary weft at the same time. The fabric still has warp rep character and the pattern warps and wefts are at intervals pulled through the warp to create the desired pattern.
(O.4373).

DOUBLE WEAVE

When two sets of warps and wefts are being woven simultaneously on the same loom a double cloth may be created. Usually the two separate layers of fabric are woven in the same technique (normally plain weave) and in two different colours. Interchanging the two layers by bringing the warp/weft set from the back of the fabric to the face and weaving it here, while weaving that from the face on the back, results in an interchange of colours and creates a two-coloured fabric.

I   II   *ill.26. Double weave. (d'Harcourt)*

This interchanging of the fabric layers binds the two simple structures into one compound fabric making it a double cloth.
(O.4155, O.4288b, C.N. 6)

The Peruvian double cloths are thus identical on the two sides, but the double-cloths can also be "incomplete" which means that one layer of fabric is not completely woven on the backside, as warps sometimes pass from one area to the next on the backside wholly or partially without being woven.

Sometimes other techniques are additionally used for patterning on a double cloth, for instance single faced brocading.(O.4288b).

In tube weaving 2 layers of complementary warp are interchanged. This was used a lot for the straps of Inca bags (O.4216).

GAUZE WEAVES

In a simple gauze weave the warps are crossed 2 by 2 before the shed is lifted and a weft interlaced in order to hold this crossing. In the next shed the warps are returned to their normal positions and the weft interlaced again. If this crossing and re-crossing is repeated with the same warps always passing in the same direction over the same adjacent ones, a structure is produced that can be identified as plain (1/1) gauze weave.
(O.4346).

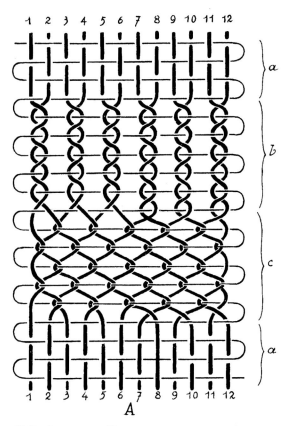

ill.27. *Gauze weave. (d'Harcourt, 1975).*

positions is called complex. The alignment of the crossing warps becomes alternating instead of vertical as the warps do not only cross and re-cross their adjacent warps, but also a number of the next to adjacent warps. In this way the warps use at least 5 wefts to come back to their original starting point. (O.D.I.c 230).

WOVEN-PILE

Woven-pile is a kind of weaving with loops or ends of yarn projecting from the plane of the fabric to form a raised surface, which tends to conceal the foundation fabric in which the yarns are concealed.

In our collection the pile-weave is a "looped pile" where the looping weft is looped around each warp and left uncut. It is used for effect in tapestry weavings like little raised squares or dots.
(O. 4139, O.4364, O.4138).

On top of a gauze weave supplementary pattern weaves (often double-faced brocade) can be made. The pattern weft is here inlaid as a weft rep, and the weaving maintains two identical sides.
(O.4170, O.4372).

Gauze weaves can be incredibly complex. A gauze weave that takes more than 2 weft rows to get the warps back to their normal

FRINGES

Many different kinds of fringes of all sizes and shapes were used in old Peru to decorate clothes. Only those occurring in the collection are mentioned here:

Warp fringes can be created by leaving the beginning and/or the end of a weaving non woven over a few or more cm, and in that way leaving the end warps hanging from the weaving like looped fringes (O.4136).

Woven fringes is another type of warp-fringe made from a tapestry woven with individual wefts every few cm, and open splits where the wefts meet.
(O.4284, O.4145).

Weft-fringes are created by letting the wefts (or some of the wefts) of a weaving extend a few cm past the selvage warp. To secure an even fringe-length during weaving, the weaver added a scaffold warp to the desired length of the fringe from the selvage warp. This scaf-

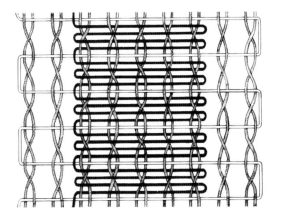

ill.28. *Gauze weave with pattern inlay. (Engelstad, 1985)*

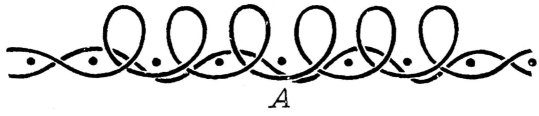

ill.29. Looped pile weave. (d'Harcourt, 1975).

fold warp was removed from the weaving after its completion.

Many of the fringes made in this technique were made on bands, where the fringes were partial – i.e. a few cm fringe, a few cm without, repeated along both, or just one, of the side selvages of the weavings. (O.4243, O.4139, O.4138).

Woven added fringes are either weft or warp fringes. A warp in the desired length and width of the fringe (usually a short, wide warp) is set up. A few cm wefts are interwoven in plain weave along the bottom selvage – just enough to keep the fringe in place. The fringes made in this technique are all left uncut in the National Museum collection. (O.4366, O. 4355, O.4151).

Weft fringes were used to make a type of "furred cord". A short fringe (0,5 cm) is cut open, and spiralled around a foundation cord. (O.D.I.c 229).

Sewn fringes. A narrow fringe was also made by spiralling a yarn around a group of cotton yarns and then sewing a row of chain stitches along the loops to hold them in place as a fringe.
(O.4349).

TASSELS

Tassels were used very much for decorating textiles. They were made by bending a group of cut yarns over a tying yarn, and then

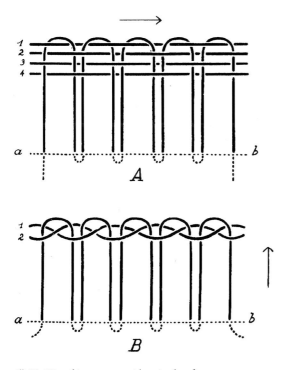

*ill.30. Warp fringe woven with twisted wefts.
(d'Harcourt, 1975).*

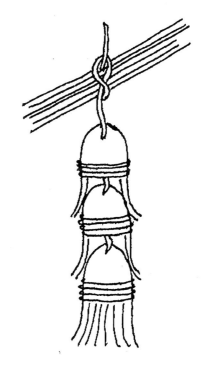

ill.31. Tassels strung together to make a furred cord.

wrapped just below the bending to hold the tassel in place. Tassels were sewn to the garments especially in the corners of bags (O.4217), along the edges of bands (O.4364) or for effect all over appliqués (O.4284, O.4139).

Tassels were also strung one on top of another to create a type of furred cord (O.5199).

APPLIQUÉS

After the fall of the Wari Empire wool became scarce along the coast and between AD 1100 and 1400 a new technique was developed: plain weave cotton material decorated with patches and bands woven in tapestry with cotton warp and woollen weft.

The bands were woven with fringes, tassels and tapestry patterns.

The patches were set up on the loom as long, narrow bands and after each patch was woven, a piece of non-woven warp was left between this and the next patch. After a long row of patches was woven, the loose warps were cut and sewn down in the weaving of each patch. These patches and bands were then sewn with cotton thread to the plain weave tunics and other weavings. Usually the patches have the same pattern on the same weaving.
(O.4137, O.4284, O.4138, O.4139).

EMBROIDERY

Accessory stitches used to decorate a fabric, whether or not the stitches also serve practical purposes, can be classified as embroidery.

RUNNING STITCH.

The running stitch is the simplest form of flat stitch in which the thread is carried forward in and out of the fabric to form a line of

stitches on each face. In Peru these stitches were used to sew together most of the fabrics, and sometimes they are seen also as a purely decorative element. (O.4141)

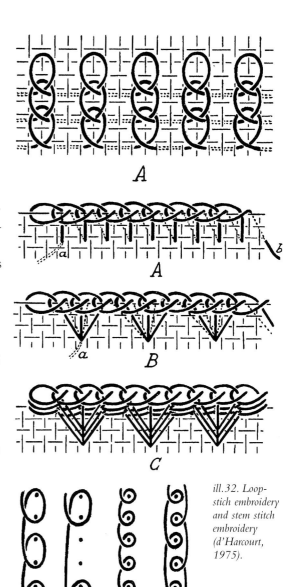

ill.32. Loop-stich embroidery and stem stitch embroidery (d'Harcourt, 1975).

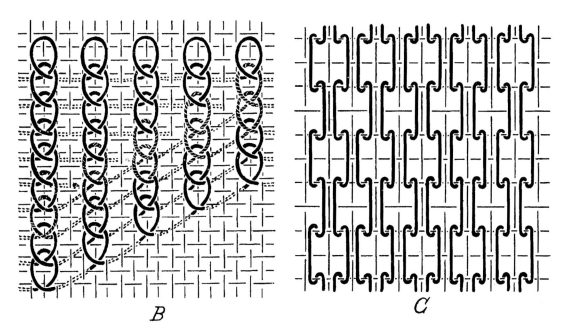

ill.33. Embroidery stitches: Loop stitches (a), loop stitches along edges (b), stem stitches (c) (d'Harcourt, 1975).

LOOP STITCH

The loop stitch resembles the chain stitch, but instead of being executed vertically, it is made in horizontal lines. In the Paracas textiles this stitch was used both sewn into a foundation fabric and also as a stitch executed partly or completely without the foundation fabric.
(H.6345, U.N.1).

Loop stitch embroidery was also used for adornment on the edges of a fabric (O.4188b) or for joining two fabrics (O.4216, O.4217).

STEM-STITCH

The stem-stitch (soumack-stitch) is a flat backstitch, which goes over twice as many

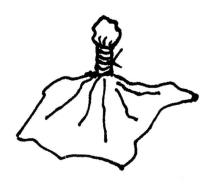

foundation cloth threads as it goes under in a circular movement.

This stitch was used mainly in southern Peru in the Paracas culture
(500 BC - 500 AD). Single lines made the earliest designs, but later it was used to completely cover the fabric. (O.6999a,b,c).

TIE DYE

Tie dye (planghi) is a method of reserve dyeing. The woven fabric (in Peru usually a light,

ill.34. Tie-dye. Ready for dyeing. The dyed textile with non dyed area where the bindings were.

loose, plain woven fabric) is at intervals gathered in small tufts that are tightly bound with a spiralling yarn. The fabric is then dyed, and after dyeing the bindings are removed. The resulting pattern consists of uncoloured circles where the bindings were. (O.4202).

PAINTING AND PRINTING

The painted textiles are made on plain-woven white or tan fabric with various brown paints and occasionally with blue paint. The painting was done with a brush made by wool, hair or plant material. Positive and negative stencils have been used. Also reserve painting has been used, where part of the fabric has been covered with a protective substance that the paint could not penetrate. The fabric has then been painted and afterwards the protective substance removed, so that the pattern would be of the original lighter colour of the fabric, and the surroundings of the darker paint. Afterwards the uncoloured areas could be painted with a lighter brown, than the surroundings (O. 4295).

Reserve paint or stencils paint: O. 4205, O.4295, O.4195.

Paint: O.4294a, c, O.4374, O.4349, O.4142, O.3037, O.4352, O.4328b.

FEATHER-MOSAIC

Many of the Peruvian fabrics were completely covered by little brightly coloured feathers from birds of the tropical rain forest.

The feathers were folded in the quill section usually over a cord, and then secured by a second cord tying a knot over each folded quill. The feathers were attached in this manner side by side, creating fringes of feathers, which were then sewn onto a plain woven non dyed cotton fabric. The stitching onto the fabric was done over the knotting yarn, and so the feather fringes were only attached at the top. Rows of feather fringes were overlapped so that the quill was hidden and the coloured part of the feathers would completely cover the foundation fabric.

Feather mantles were often used as the outmost cover of the mummies. Their ornamentation often takes the form of monochrome horizontal or oblique bands of varying widths (O.6789, O.6790) but occasionally the feathers form a polychrome design, which can be very complex (O.6712).

CROSS REFERENCES

One element:
Looping: O.10.267, O.10.268
Loopstitch: U.N.1, H. 6345
Peruke stitch: C.N. 6

Two elements:
Cord wrapping: O.10.271, O.4032
Flat double wrap: O.10.267, O.10.268, O.4030

One set of elements:
Braiding: O.D.I.c 204, O.4256
Warp-braiding: O.4136
Sprang: O.10.319

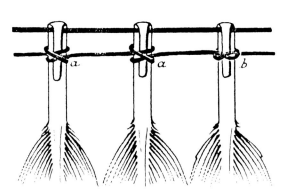

ill.35. Feathers arranged in rows for feather-mosaics. (d'Harcourt, 1975).

WEAVING

Plain weave: O.D.I.c 236a, O.D.I.c 267, O.4131, O.4136

Discontinous warp: O.10.276, O.4333, O.4170

Shaped warp: O.4325c

Tapestry: C.N. 0, O.4131, O.4137, O.4145, O.4174, O.4217, O.4231, O.4237, O.4243, O.4251, O.4277, O.4281, O.4284, O.4311, O.4325, O.4326, O.4331, O.4346, O.4366, O.4407a, O.5199

Warp rep patterning: C.N.10, O.4216, C.N.12, O.4301a.

Complementary weft weave with substituting colours:
C.N. 0, O.4151, O.4188b, O.4238, O.4355

Supplementary weaves.
Brocade: O.3032, O.4151, O.4170, O.4298, O.4299, O.4340a, O.4369, O.4372, O.4399, O.5674

Supplementary warp patterning: O.4193, O.4223.

Supplementary warp and weft patterning: O.4373

Double weave: C.N.6, O.4155, O.4288

Gauze weave: O.D.I.c 230, O.4170, O.4346, O.4372

Decoration of fabrics:
Tassels, fringes, pile: O.4238, O.4139, O.4364, O.D.I.c.229, O.5659
Embroidery: O.4141, O.6999
Application: O.4137
Feather mosaic: O.6712, O.6789, O.6790

Painted fabrics: O.3037, O.4142, O.4195, O.4205, O.4294, O.4295, O.4328, O.4349, O.4352, O.4374
Tie dye: O.4202

LITERATURE:

Ayala, Guaman Poma de (1936) *El Primer Nueva Cronica y Buen Gobierno* (1615), Paris: Travaux et Memoires de l'Institut d'Ethnologie XXIII, Université de Paris.

Anthon, Ferdinand (1984) *Altindianische Textilkunst aus Peru*, Leipzig: A.Seemann Verlag.

Arte Mayor de los Andes, Santiago: Museo Chileno de Arte Precolombino. (1989)

Becher, H. (1978) *Die präcolumbische Peru-Sammlung Gretzer in der Völkerkundeabteilung des Niersächsischen Landesmuseums Hannover,* Amerikanistische Studien I, Festschriff Trimborn, St.Augustin.

Bjerregaard, Lena (1976) *Indianervævning fra Guatemala,* København: Høst & Søn.

Bjerregaard, L.(1996) *Arkæologiske peruanske tekstiler på Nationalmuseet.* Conference paper, Fuglsø Museumsmøde.

Bird, Junius (1986), *The Junius B.Bird Conference on Andean Textiles* in 1984, Textile Museum Washington.

Bird, Junius B. and Hyslop, John (1985) *The preceramic excavations at the Huaca Prieta Chicama Valley, Peru,* New York: American Museum of Natural History.

Bosqued, C.B. and Gomez, L.J.R. (1980) *Los Tejidos Prehispanicos del Area Central Andina en el Museo de America,* Lima: Ministerio de Cultura, Lima.

Burger, Richard (1992) *Chavin and the Origins of Andean Civilization,* Thames and Hudson

Cieza de Leon, Pedro (1862 (1550)) *Primera Parte de la Cronica del Peru, in Biblioteca de Autores Españoles, 2 voll., Madrid.*

Conklin, W.J.(1971) *Chavin Textiles and the Origin of Peruvian Weaving,*in: Textile Museum Journal, p.13-19, Washington D.C..

Easby, E. (1966) *Conservation of an Unique Peruvian Fabric* in: Brooklyn Museum Annual, vol.VII, p.65-73, Brooklyn Museum.

Ekroth-Edebo, M. (1988*) Peruanska Textileren teknisk undersökning,* Göteborgs Universitet, Institutionen för Kulturvård.

Eisleb, D.and Strelow,R. (1964) *Altperuanische kelim-gewebe aus den Sammlungen des Berliner Museums für Völkerkunde,* Baessler Archiv 12, p.257-270, Berlin:Verlag von Dietrich Reimer.

Eisleb, D. and Strelow, R. (1966) *Altperuanische unechte partialgewebe mit plangimusterung,* Baessler Archiv 13, p.293-308, Berlin:Verlag von Dietrich Reimer.

Emery, Irene (1966) *The Primary Structures of Fabrics,*Washington D.C.:Textile Museum.

Irene Emery Roundtable on Museum Textiles, Archaeological Textiles, 1974 *Etnographic Textiles of the Western Hemisphere,* 1976.

Engelstad, Helen (1990) *A group of Grave tablets from Pachacamac,* Nawpa Pacha 24, 23 pages, Institute of Andean Studies, Berkeley.

Engelstad, Helen (1984*) Mythology, Religion, and Textile Art on the Central Coast of Old Peru,* Folk ol.26, p.191-217.

Engelstad, Helen (1985) *Vævningerer fra det gamle Peru,* København: Nationalmuseet.

Gohl E.P.G. and Vilensky L.D. (1983) *Textile Science,* Melbourne: Longman Chesire.

Frame, Mary (1986) *Nasca Sprang tassels: Struc-*

ture, Technique and order, The Textile Museum Journal, p.67 - 77, Washington D.C.

d'Harcourt, Raoul (1975) *Textiles of ancient Peru and their Techniques*, London: University of Washington Press.

Isacsson, Svend-Erik (1994) *Man of Fibre: The Paracas Fabrics in Native Tradition of Western South America,* Acta Americana, vol.2, Nr.2, p.27-41, Svenska Amerikanist -selskabet, Uppsala Universitet, Uppsala.

King, M.E. (1956) *A premilinary study of a shaped textile from Peru* in: Workshop Notes, paper no 13, Textile Museum, Washington D.C.

King, M.E. (1968) *Some new Paracas Textile Techniques from Ocucaje, Peru* in: Verhandlungen des XXXVIII Internationalen Amerikanisten kongresses, Stuttgard-Munic: K.Renner.

Los textiles precolombinos y su conservacion, Lima: Proyecto Regional de Patrimonio Cultural PNUD/UNESCO.

Murra, John V. (1958) *La Funcion del Tejido en Varios Contextos Sociales y Politicos*, Lima: Instituto de Estudios Peruanos.

Montell, Gösta (1929) *Dress and Ornament in Ancient Peru*, archaeological and historical studies, Göteborg: Elanders.

Olsen Bruhns, Karen (1994) *Ancient South America*, Cambridge World Archaeology, Cambridge University Press.

O'Neale, L.M. (1934) *Peruvian needleknitting* in: American Anthropologist 36, p.405-431.

Paul, Anne (1979) *Paracas Textiles*, Göteborg: Göteborgs Etnografiska Museum.

Reeves, Pat (1968) *Conservation of a Peruvian Paracas Acropolis Mantle*, Curator XI, p.21-25.

Rowe, Ann P. (1971) *Interlocking warp and weft in the Nasca 2 Style*, Textile Museum Journal, p.67-78, Washington D.C.

Rowe, Ann P. (1992) *Provincial Inca Tunics of the South Coast of Peru* Textile Museum Journal, p.5-51, Washington D.C.

Rowe, J.R. (1972) *Standardization in Inca Tapestry Tunics*, Univ. of California, p.239-64, Berkeley.

Rowe, Ann P. (1984) *Costumes and Featherwork of the Lords of Chimor*, Washington D.C.: Textile Museum.

Rowe, Ann P. (1992) *Warp patterned weaves of the Andes*, Washington D.C.: Textile Museum.

Seiler-Baldinger, Annemarie (1994) *Textiles – a Classification of Techniques*, Washington D.C.: Smithsonian Institution Press.

van Stan, I. (1967) *Textiles from beneath the temple of Pachacamac*, Museum Monographs, Philedelphia: University of Pennesylvania.

Stone-Miller, Rebecca (1992) *To weave for the Sun*, Boston: Museum of Fine Arts.

Strelov, Renate (1996) *Gewebe mit unterbrochenen Ketten aus dem Vorspanischen Peru*, Berlin: Museum für Völkerkunde Neue Folge 61, Abteilung Amerikanische Archaologie X.

Strömberg, Geijer, Hald, Hoffmann (1974) *Nordisk textilteknisk terminologi,* Oslo: Johan Grunt Tanum Forlag.

Uhle, Max and Shimada, Izumi (1991) *Pachacamac, a reprint of the 1903 edition,* Philadelphia: University of Pennesylvania.

Wildman, A.B. (1954) *The microscopy of Animal Fibers*, Bradford: Land Humphries.

The Textiles

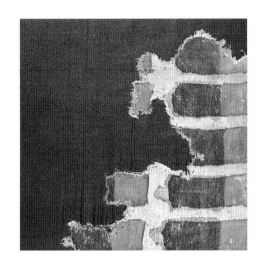

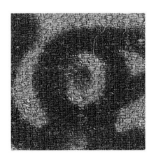

THE TEXTILES

Key for understanding the charts:
Warp is ALWAYS mentioned before weft
(by size or other).

Provenience or date in brackets are estimated by the
author.

The state of condition (estimated by the author)
is expressed in numbers from 1-5
(5 being the most brittle).
sg.ply means: single ply.
mm under fibre analysis refers to the diameter of the
yarns in question.
Technical terms are according to Irene Emery (1966),
Seiler–Baldinger (1994) and d'Harcourt (1975).
See literature reference.

🐾 indicates warp direction

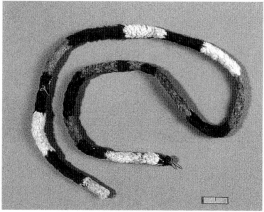

Mus. No.: O.D.I.c 204
Type: Head band
Material: Wool
Technique: Braiding
Colour: Green, brown
Provenience: Trujillo (according to collector)
Size: 3 x 55 cm
Date: Unknown
Cross-reference: O.4256

Description
The head band is braided from 24 strands: 6 brown, 6 green, 6 brown, 6 green. Each strand is made up of two threads. The weaving is a little loose, so the two colours can be seen, where they meet. The braided band is fastened around a "false mummy's head"– a cloth bundle in the shape of a head, which was put on top of the wrapped mummy. This head is made from red plain weave wool (2 ply, S twist) and is stuffed with plant material and pieces of woven textiles. The head is decorated with human hair, the nose is made out of wood and the eyes from shells with a piece of black clay with textile imprint for the iris.

Fibre Analysis
The braid is from 2 ply S, wool, 1,8 mm, condition 3.
The wool has very many scales.
pH wool 3,2.

Acquired by:
From Wiener's collection. Acquired by the National Museum in 1882.

Mus. No.: O.D.I.c 229
Type: Furred cord (fragment)
Material: Wool and cotton
Technique: Woollen fringes wrapped in spiral around a cord
Colour: Yellow, red, black
Provenience: Cajamarca (according to collector)
Size: 66 x 0,9 cm
Date: Unknown
Cross-reference: O.10271, O.10277

Description
A woollen fringe is woven, the fringe wool being the weft, and the warp being two twisted cotton strings. The woollen weft is then cut at the far end of the weft and the fringe is spiralled around a foundation cord of cotton, held in place at irregular intervals by stitches with cotton thread. The cord is only a fragment and broken in both ends, so it is not possible to know what purpose it served.

Fibre Analysis
Cotton core: 2 ply S, cotton, 0,4 mm, condition 5.
Weft: 2 ply S, wool, 1,5 mm, condition 5.
pH wool 5,8.

Acquired by:
From Wiener's collection. Acquired by the National Museum in 1882.

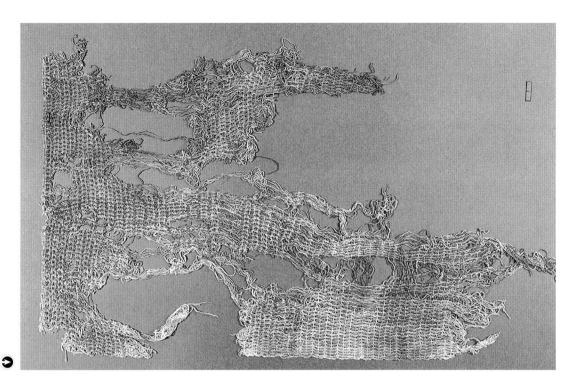

Mus. No.: O.D.I.c 230
Type: Fragment
Material: Cotton
Technique: Gauze weave
Colour: Blue, tan
Provenience: Ancon
Size: 58 x 32 cm
Date: 1100 – 1450 AD
Technical Explanation: Complex gauze
Cross-reference: O.4170, O.4346, O.4372

Description

The textile fragment has a selvage at one end of the warp. The warp is: one round blue, one round white /tan. The warp knots must be at the opposite end of the warp (no longer existing).

The wefts alternate between a white and a blue thread. The white weft goes over 1 under 1 warp, and the blue weft over 2 under 2 warps.

The gauze report is completed over 5 wefts.

Fibre Analysis

The thread count is 12 x 2 per cm.
Warp: 2 ply S, cotton, 0,6 mm, condition 3.
Weft: 2 ply S, cotton, 1 mm, condition 3.
pH cotton 6,6.

Acquired by:

From Wiener's collection. Stated to be from Ancon. Acquired by the National Museum in 1882

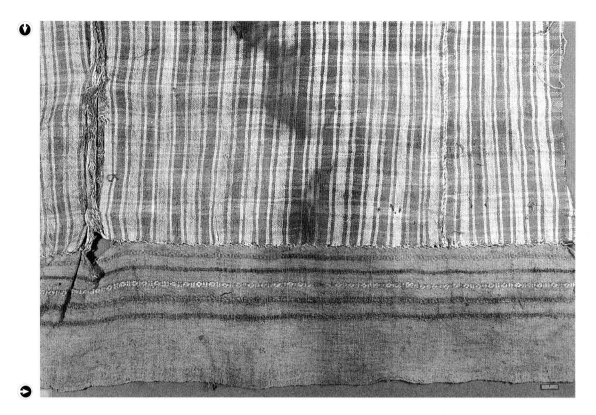

Mus. No. O.D.I.c 236a
Type: Cloth
Material: Cotton
Technique: Plain weave with supplementary warp patterning
Colour: White and tan with warp patterns in blue/tan/white/brown
Provenience: Ancon (Chimu)
Size: 240 x 79 cm
Date: 1100 - 1450 AD
Cross-reference: O.D.I.c 267, O..4131, O.4136

Description

The textile consists of a complete checker panel measuring 67 x 207 cm and with four selvages. To this is sewn a similar panel of the same length, but which has been cut to only 16 cm width.

At either end of the fabric is sewn a 33 cm wide monochrome tan plain weave panel with four 6 mm wide stripes in supplementary warp patterning.

The warp in one of the border bands is changing its spinning direction (6 cm Z twist, 1 cm both S and Z, the rest S twist).

Fibre analysis:

The plain weave is 2 warps/ one weft in both the attached band and in the middle piece. The band has 12 warps and 9 wefts per cm. The checker middle piece has 16 warps and 11 wefts per cm.

Fibre Analysis

The middle piece has 16 x 11 threads per cm and both warp and weft of sg.ply S cotton.
The border has 12 x 9 threads per cm.
The border weft is in sg.ply S weft.
The border warp is sg.ply, but the twist is both S and Z.
The pattern warp: blue and tan – sg.ply Z; brown and white – sg.ply S.
All threads are 0,4 -5 mm, condition 1.
pH cotton warp 5,5.
pH cotton weft 6,5.
Surface pH 5,2.

Acquired by:

From Charnay's collection. Acquired by the National Museum in 1882.

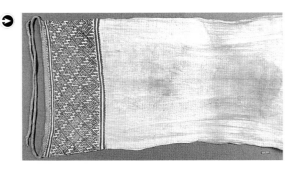

Mus. No.: O.3032
Type: Breechcloth
Material: Cotton
Technique: Plain weave with 2 faced selvage to selvage brocade (lancé)
Colour: White, brown
Provenience: Chancay
Size: 108 x 34 cm
Date: 800 - 1400 AD
Cross-reference: O.4151, O.4170, O.5674, O.4340a

Description

The breechcloth is complete with 4 selvages and tying belt. It is woven in plain weave with a 13 cm wide brocaded band along one end. The selvage to selvage pattern is purely geometric and always has 2 or 4 warp threads in each pattern unit. This makes the pattern 2 sided – where the warps are uncovered in the front, they are covered with the pattern weft in the back; and vice versa.

The brocaded band is edged top and bottom by 3 stripes of 0,2-5 cm (brown, white, brown) in weft rep with 4 warps of the plain weave in each shed. At the end of the brocaded band is sewn a 1 cm wide warp rep plain weave band for tying the breechcloth. The loose warps at each end of this belt are gathered in 3 bundles and braided.

Fibre Analysis

The plain weave has 18 warps and 12 wefts per cm.
Warp: sg.ply S, cotton, 0,2-4 mm, condition 2.
Weft: sg.ply Z, cotton, 0,2-4 mm, condition 2.
Pattern weft: 2 ply S, cotton, 0,4-8 mm, condition 1.
pH plain weave cotton 7,3.

Acquired by:

From dr. Gafron's collection. Bought from Gothenburg Museum in 1921. The remaining collection is Gothenburg.

Mus. No.: O.D.I.c 267
Type: Scarf
Material: Cotton
Technique: Plain weave
Colour: White
Provenience: Trujillo (Chimu)
Size: 51 x 51 cm
Date: 1000 - 1400 AD
Cross-reference: O.D.1.c 236a, O.4131, O.4136, O.4202

Description

A square textile loosely woven in plain weave, and with four selvages. At the top and bottom of the warp are 3 rows of double wefts. At each corner one or two of these double wefts are left to hang loose, as a corner tuft.

Almost at the center of the textile a small tuft of non spun, brown cotton is looped around two warps.

Fibre Analysis

The thread count is 3-4 warps and 2-3 wefts per cm.
Both warp and weft are 2 ply S cotton, 1,8 mm, condition 1.
pH cotton 8,6.

Acquired by:

Acquired by the National Museum in 1894 with the following note: "Traded from Prof. H.H. Gigliole in Florentz for ethnografica and Nordic antiquities."

Mus. No.: O.3037
Type: Fragment
Material: Cotton
Technique: Plain weave with painting
Colour: White with tan painting
Provenience: The coast of Peru
Size: 47 x 50 cm
Date: Unknown
Cross-reference: O.4142, O.4379, O.4294

Description

The weaving has selvage along one side. The other three sides are cut off.

The pattern is painted on and is of very great variation. There are birds, fish and geometric figures.

Fibre Analysis

The weaving is a warp rep and has 7 wefts and 20 warps per cm.
Both warp and weft are 2 ply S, cotton, 0,5 mm, condition 1.
pH cotton 6,6.

Acquired by:

From Dr. Gafron's collection; a German doctor, who worked in Lima. Bought in 1921 from Gothenburg's Museum, where the remaining collection is kept.

Mus. No.: O.4030
Type: Bag decoration piece
Material: Wool, cotton
Technique: Flat double wrap
Colour: Red, yellow, black, white
Provenience: Ica
Size: 13 x 5,5 - 20 cm, fringe 16 cm
Date: Unknown
Cross-reference: O.10267, O.10268

Description

Coarse cotton yarns are stretched horizontally according to the desired shape of the textile in two identical layers. The yarns of each layer are joined to each other vertically by stem- stitch embroidery with wool yarns. At certain points the yarns alternate passing from one side to the other, as in double weaving. This technique produces a thick and stiff fabric with ornamental motives the same on the two sides but with reversed colour values.

Fibre Analysis

The wool used here is 2 ply S, 0,5 mm, condition 1.
The inner cotton is sg.ply S, 1 mm, condition 5.
The fringe is 2 ply S, 0,5 mm, condition 1.
pH wool 4,4.
pH cotton 5,9.

Surface pH wool 4,5.
The 16 cm fringe is made up of woollen yarns twisted together with looped ends. It is sewn to the textile.

Acquired by:

From the Gretzer collection. Acquired by the National Museum in 1923 from the Museum für Völkerkunde, Berlin.

Mus. No.: O.4032
Type: Sling
Material: Cotton, wool
Technique: Cord wrapping with embroidery, braiding
Colour: Light brown, dark brown, red, white
Provenience: Ica
Size: 360 cm length – diameter 1-2,5 cm – width of middle part 7 cm. Middle part 48 x 35 cm fringes.
Date: Unknown
Cross-reference: O.5659

Description

The middle part of the sling (15 cm) is sewn over a cotton yarn foundation, which is spread out, like plain weave weft rep. In the middle is a 5 cm long slit, and along the sides are stem stitch embroidery. At either end the foundation yarns are gathered and wrapped with a cotton cord into a cylindrical form 17 cm long and 2,5 cm in diameter and embroidered with stem stitch. The foundation yarn is reduced and woollen threads in two alternating colours are braided in a cylinder for the 155 cm long, 1 cm wide cord, which ends in a 30 cm fringe made by the loose hanging braiding yarns twisted together so that each fringe-yarn has two colours.

Fibre Analysis

The embroidery is made in wool (beige, red, dark brown) and a white cotton.
Wool, 2 ply S, 0.4 mm, condition 3.
Cotton, 2 ply S, 0,4 mm, condition 3.
pH wool 3,6.
Surface pH wool 4,3.

Acquired by:

From the Gretzer collection. Acquired by the National Museum in 1923 from the Museum für Völkerkunde, Berlin.

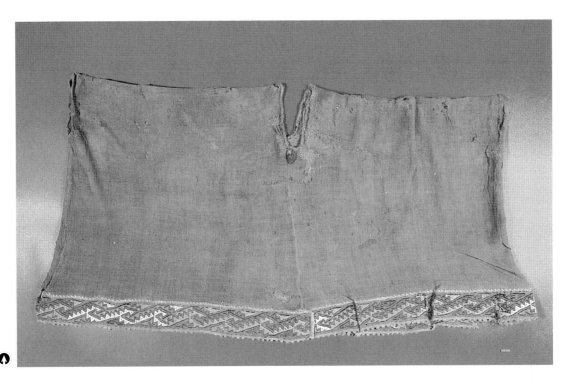

Mus. No.: O.4131
Type: Tunic
Material: Cotton, wool
Technique: Plain weave, tapestry
Colour: Tan. Tapestry band: tan, rose, sky blue, black, green, curry
Provenience: Pachacamac
Size: 43 x 98 cm
Date: 800 - 1200 AD
Technical Explanation: 1. Plain weave
2. Tapestry with slits, 3. Loop stitch embroidery
Cross-reference: O.4131, C.N.0, O.4343

Description
A complete tunic, loosely woven of very fine single ply cotton threads. It is sewn together from two identical pieces (width: 49 cm, length 76 cm). At the neck a 20 cm long slit is left open and bordered by 5 rows of loop stitch embroidery. A small red tassel is placed at one end of the neck slit, it is probably the front. The sides are sewn together and a 10 cm long opening left for armholes.
At the bottom of the tunic a 5 cm wide tapestry woven band is attached. It has a small fringe at the bottom side consisting of 3 mm wefts protruding from the weaving over 5 mm with 5 mm in between. The tapestry band is double over 32 cm, and thus measures 5 x 228 cm. It must have been made not especially for this tunic but have been a recycle item, and as textiles were most often not cut it was doubled to fit this tunic.

Fibre Analysis
The plain weave tunica has 20 warps and 16 wefts per cm.
Both warp and weft are sg.ply S, cotton, 0,2 mm, condition 3.
The tapestry weaving has 9 warps and 32 wefts per cm.
The tapestry warp is 3 ply Z, cotton, 0,4 mm, condition 3.
The tapestry weft is 2 ply S, wool, 0,5 mm, condition 1.
The neck embroidery is sewn with 4 strands of 2 ply S wool, condition 1.

Acquired by:
From the Gretzer collection. Acquired by the National Museum in 1922 from the Museum für Völkerkunde, Berlin.

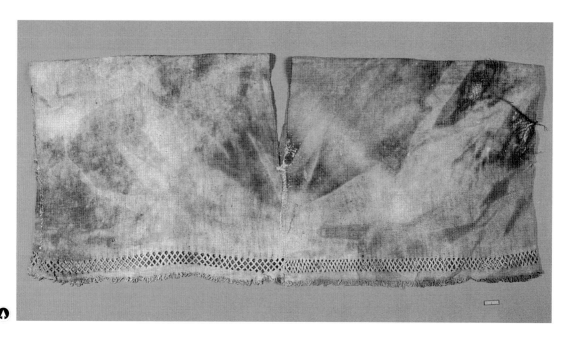

Mus. No.: O.4136
Type: Tunic
Material: Cotton
Technique: Plain weave and warp plaiting (a-jour)
Colour: Tan
Provenience: Pachacamac
Size: 29 x 69 cm
Date: 800 – 1200 AD
Cross-reference: O.D.I.c 236a, O.4136

Description

The plain woven tunic is made from two panels sewn together mid front. At the bottom is a 5 cm wide plaited openwork part, plaited by the warp threads: 8 warp threads are separated, the two outer ones twice woven through the 6 remaining warps. The group of 8 warps is then divided in two, each one woven with 4 warps of the neighbouring warp group, and so forth.

The bottom of the tunic has a one cm uncut fringe, consisting of the loose warp ends of the textile.

Fibre Analysis

The weaving has 14 warps and 10 wefts per cm. Both warp and weft are 2 ply S, cotton, 0,5 mm, condition 4.
pH cotton 5,5.

Acquired by:

From the Gretzer collection. Acquired by the National Museum in 1923 from the Museum für Völkerkunde, Berlin.

Mus. No.: O.4137
Type: Tunic (fragment)
Material: Cotton
Technique: Plain weave, tapestry, application
Colour: Foundation: white
Applications: white, blue, green, 2 browns, olive
Provenience: Pachacamac
Size: 87 x 129 cm
Date: 1100 - 1400 AD
Cross-reference: O.4139, O.4284

Description

Tunic woven in loose plain weave cotton.

The tunic has tapestry woven bands sewn vertically between the 4 plain weave panels – one band in the middle with a neck slit of 18 cm (62 cm from the bottom edge – so the total length of the tunic was 71 cm) – two at 55 cm from the middle and one horizontally at the bottom of the tunic. A similar tapestry woven band is sewn horizontally to the tunic at the place, where the neck slit starts, and to one side.

The tunic has appliquéd tapestry woven squares of ca 8,5 x 14 cm sewn on at regular intervals. These tapestry woven pieces have weft selvages, but are cut top and bottom – so they were woven in bands with a little unwoven warp in between and the warp was then cut between the woven squares. The loose warp-ends were then sewn into the fabric. The motives are ducks.

Fibre Analysis

The plain woven fabric has 12 warps and 11 wefts per cm.
Warp and weft: sg.ply S, cotton, 0,4 mm, condition 3.
The tapestry has 8 warps and 20 wefts per cm.
Warp: sg.ply S, cotton, 0,3-6 mm (uneven), condition 3.
Weft: sg.ply S and Z cotton, 0,3-6 (uneven), condition 3.
Sewing thread: 2 ply Z, cotton, 0,4 mm, condition 3.
pH plain weave cotton, 6,7.

Acquired by:

From the Gretzer collection. Acquired by the National Museum in 1923 from the Museum für Völkerkunde, Berlin.

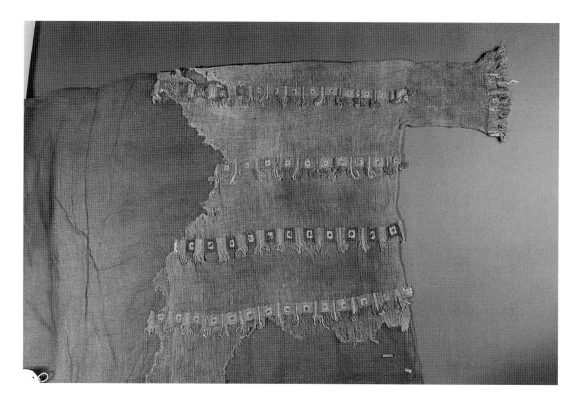

Mus. No.: O.4138
Type: Shirt (fragment)
Material: Cotton, wool
Technique: Loose plain weave with tapestry woven bands, fringes and pile
Colour: Tan, two browns, blue, yellow
Provenience: Pachacamac
Size: 70 x 65 cm
Date: 1100 - 1400 AD
Cross-reference: O.4139

Description

Fragment of a shirt with small, narrow sleeves (20 cm long, 13 cm wide) sewn to the very wide shirt body, so the sleeves function almost like cuffs.

The shirt material is plain woven cotton and the 2 cm wide tapestry bands are sewn on for decoration. The bands have narrow stripes. Each 2 cm the weft is prolonged for 2 x 2 cm long fringes. Between the fringes are little squares with loop pile weaving.

Fibre Analysis

Foundation cloth: 8 warp x 8 wefts per cm.
Warp: sg.ply S, cotton, 0,4mm, condition 3.
Weft: sg.ply S, cotton, 0,4mm, condition 3.
Tapestry bands: 9 warps x 15 wefts per cm.
Warp: sg.ply S, cotton, 0,3mm, condition 3.
Weft: sg.ply S and 2 ply S, wool, 0,4-1 mm, condition 1.
Sewing: 2 ply Z, cotton, 0,6mm, condition 1.
pH cotton 5,7.
pH wool 5,9.

Acquired by:

From the Gretzer collection. Acquired by the National Museum in 1923 from the Museum für Völkerkunde, Berlin.

Mus. No.: O.4139
Type: Shirt (fragmemt)
Material: Foundation: cotton. Decoration: wool
Technique: Plain weave; tapestry, pile, fringes and tassels appliquéd on to the foundation cloth
Colour: Foundation: brown. Decoration: red, yellow, blue
Provenience: Pachacamac
Size: 63 x 145 cm
Date: 1100 – 1400 AD
Cross-reference: O.4138

Description

Shirt made from loosely woven plain weave cotton material decorated with tapestry woven fringy ribbons sewn on to the shirt horizontally and vertically producing a checker effect. From the horizontally placed ribbons little tasselled men with big headdresses are hanging. The shirt is sewn from two probably similar pieces, and the sleeves (20 x 19 cm) are sewn on.

The tapestry ribbons are sewn on to the fabric with 1 cm big cross stitches between each fringe part.

Little men are hanging from a tapestry woven band. They consist of a tapestry woven fringe band themselves and have a big headdress consisting of a curved tapestry woven fringe – only to one side – band; woven straight and curved when sewn on. They are decorated with many red tassels.

Fibre Analysis

The thread count is 5 warps and 5 wefts per cm. The foundation threads are 2 ply S, cotton, 0,4 mm, condition 3.
The tapestry warp: sg.ply S, cotton, 0,6 mm, condition 3.
The tapestry weft: sg.ply S, wool, 0,8 mm, condition 3.
2 ply Z, cotton 0,6 mm, condition 3.
pH cotton 5,8.
pH red wool 4,7.

Acquired by:

From the Gretzer collection. Acquired by the National Museum in 1922 from the Museum für Völkerkunde, Berlin.

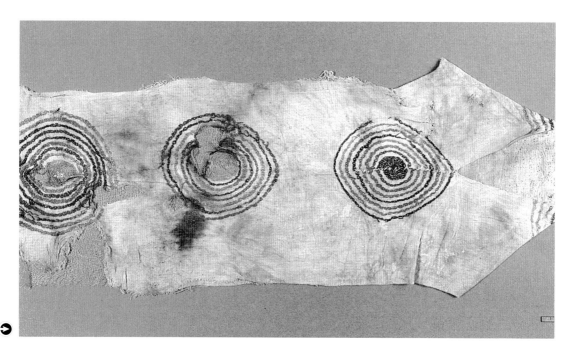

Mus. No.: O.4141
Type: Fragment
Material: Cotton and wool
Technique: Cotton weave with wool embroidery and plain weave, (2/1) with running stitch embroidery
Colour: Brown undyed cotton with embroidery in blue, yellow, red and green wool
Size: 168 x 13 cm
Date: Unknown
Cross-reference: O.4131

Description

The textile is a long narrow piece of plain weave (2 warp/ 1 weft) cut along one side and at the two ends. The other side is a selvage. The textile is doubled and sewn together along the selvage side except for 36 cm in the middle.

It is embroidered with 4 multicoloured circle patterns along the sewn seam and one semicircle in the middle of the open middle section.

Fibre Analysis

The thread count is 12 warps and 11 wefts per cm.

Warp and weft are sg.ply S, cotton, 0,2 mm, condition 2.

The pattern yarn is 2 ply S, wool, 0,6 mm, condition 1.

pH cotton 6,9.

Acquired by:

From the Gretzer collection. Acquired by the National Museum in 1923 from the Museum für Völkerkunde, Berlin.

Mus. No.: O.4142
Type: Fragment
Material: Cotton
Technique: Plain weave and painting
Colour: Light tan fabric with brown paint
Provenience: Pachacamac
Size: 63 x 35 cm
Date: 800-1200 AD
Cross-reference: O.495, O.4328

Description

The upper 25 cm of the fragment is folded and sewn along the edge leaving a 7 cm opening at the top. The sewing thread is probably not original judged from its grip and state of conservation as seen in the microscope.

There is fragments of running stitches along the slanting edge of the fabric – these seem to be original, but their use cannot be ascertained.

The textile has selvage along the shortest edge and the longest side edge. The other sides are cut.

The design shows running birds.

Fibre Analysis

The weaving is 2/2 plain weave, with 14 warps and 9 wefts per cm.

The warp is sg.ply Z, cotton, 0,3-4 mm, condition 1.
The weft is sg.ply S, cotton, 0,3-4 mm, condition 1.
The running stitches are two strands of 2 ply S twist (Z,S,Z), cotton, condition 1.
The blue sewing thread is 4 strands of 2 ply, S twist (Z,S,Z),cotton, condition 1.
pH cotton 6,2.

Acquired by:

From the Gretzer collection. Acquired by the National Museum in 1922

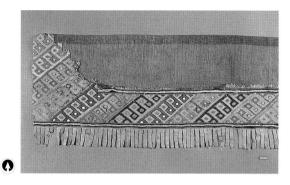

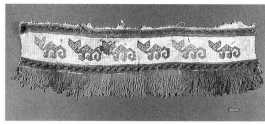

Mus. No.: O.4145
Type: Woven fringe
Material: Wool
Technique: Tapestry
Colour: Yellow, red, black, pink, curry, white
Provenience: Pachacamac
Size: 121 x 10-24 cm
Date: 800 - 1200 AD
Technical Explanation: Tapestry with long vertical slits for fringes
Cross-reference: O.4281, O.4284, O.4366c

Description

The textile is probably the bottom part of a tunic. The fringe is woven in tapestry, with long vertical slits. The fringes have been cut at 8 cm 's length; they are 2 cm wide.

Soumack wrapping is used for contours in the tapestry. The textile is sewn together from 2 pieces 10 cm wide, and in the left corner it is extended upwards in a step-fret pattern to 24 cm's width. The textile has narrow fragments of a plain weave at the top and has been cut off along the top side. The tapestry has two warps of the plain weaving in each warp shed – thus being a weft rep 2/2 across the plain weave.

Fibre Analysis

Tapestry 6 warps x 16 wefts per cm.
Warp: 2 ply S, cotton, 0,4mm, condition 5.
Weft: 2 ply S, wool, 0,5mm, condition 3.
Plain weave: 6 warps x 8 wefts per cm.
Warp/weft: 2 ply S, cotton, 0,5mm, condition 3.
pH warp cotton 6,6.
pH weft wool 3,5.

Acquired by:

From the Gretzer collection. Acquired by the National Museum in 1922 from the Museum für Völkerkunde, Berlin.

Mus. No.: O.4151
Type: Band with fringe
Material: Wool and cotton
Technique: Two faced brocading and complementary weft weaving
Colour: White plain weave with decoration in tan, yellow and red
Provenience: Pachacamac
Size: 46 x 13 cm
Date: Approx. 800-1200 AD
Technical Explanation: Two faced brocading, complementary weft with substituting colours, weft rep plain weave, fringe
Cross-reference: O.41886, O.4170

Description

A band with 3 selvages and a 5 cm fringe along the bottom warp selvage – probably the bottom part of a panel of a tunica. The decoration of the band is a row of cats in different colours. Over and under the cats are 1 cm wide weft rep stripes. Between the rep stripes is a pattern in complementary weft weave with substituting colours.

The fringe is an added uncut warp woven with 6 wefts along one side to hold the warp-fringes in place.

The design shows feline animals.

Fibre Analysis

Plain weave:
The plain weave has per cm 17 warps and 12 wefts.
Warp, 2 ply S, cotton, 0,3-4 mm, condition 1.
Weft 2 ply S, cotton, 0,3-4 mm, condition 1.
Pattern weft: 2 strands of sg.ply Z, wool, 0,5 mm, condition 1.
Fringe, 2 ply S, wool, 1,0 mm, condition 1.
pH cotton warp/weft 7,0.

Acquired by:

From the Gretzer collection. Acquired by the National Museum in 1923 from the Museum für Völkerkunde, Berlin.

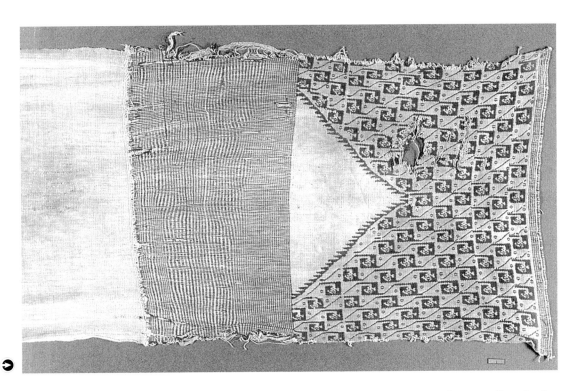

Mus. No.: O.4155
Type: Breechcloth
Material: Cotton
Technique: Double weave, plain weave
Colour: White, brown
Provenience: Pachacamac
Size: 33 x 252 cm
Date: 800 - 1200 AD
Cross-reference: O.4288, C.N.6

Description

Breechcloth consisting of two pieces of weavings each with selvages on all 4 sides, and joined together by sewing.

One piece is plain weave and measures 204 x 33 cm.

The other piece (48 x 33 cm) (for folding down in the front) is double weave. The bottom 1 cm and the top 17,5 cm are horizontally striped in warp rep plain weave 2/2.

Between the stripes the warp is separated by two layers of different colour and woven in double weave in a pattern of little squares with bird motifs. In the middle a triangular monochrome piece.

Fibre Analysis

The plain weave has 11 warps and 20 wefts per cm.
Warp: 2 ply S, cotton, 0,6 mm, condition 3.
Weft: 2 ply S, cotton, 0,6 mm, condition 3.
The double weave has 19 warps and 12 wefts per cm.
Warp: 2 ply S, cotton, 0,5 mm, condition 3.
Weft: 2 ply S, cotton, 0,5 mm, condition 3.
pH warp cotton 6,6.
PH weft cotton 6,7.

Acquired by:

From the Gretzer collection. Acquired by the National Museum in 1922 from the Museum für Völkerkunde, Berlin.

Mus. No.: O.4170
Type: Fragment
Material: Cotton
Technique: Gauze weave, brocading, discontinuous warp and weft
Colour: Foundation: brown and tan. Tan, brown, white and blue patterning
Provenience: Pachacamac
Size: 80 x 68 cm
Date: 800 – 1200 AD
Cross-reference: O.D.I.c 230, O.4399, O.43336

Description

The fragment consists of two pieces sewn together along the side selvages. Part of the two side selvages exist on both textiles, and a little bit of the top (or bottom) selvage on one of them. The warp is discontinuous, the two warp sets in each weaving (brown and tan) are interlocked around a scaffold weft, which is still there, and which has been used to sew the warps together along the vertical slits in the step-fret pattern.

The weaving is simple gauze weave, where the same two warps cross each other between each weft. Where the step pattern is, the foundation weft is discontinuous, being brown in the brown warp and tan in the tan.

A brocaded pattern picturing a person is regularly spread over the brown part of the textile. Little fragments of similar brocading can be seen in the tan part of the textile; these are bird designs. The brocading is double sided – inlaid as a weft rep with an interlocked warp pair in each shed.

Fibre Analysis

The thread count is 12 warps and 4 wefts per cm. All threads are 2 ply S, cotton, 0,4 mm, condition 4.
There is a lot of "dead cotton" (unripe cotton) among the fibres.
pH dark cotton 6,8.
pH light cotton 6,8.

Acquired by:

From the Gretzer collection. Acquired by the National Museum in 1923 from the Museum für Völkerkunde, Berlin.

Mus. No.: O.4174
Type: Fragment
Material: Wool, cotton
Technique: Dovetailed tapestry
Colour: Red, green, 2 browns, white
Provenience: Pachacamac
Size: 84 x 75
Date: 1000 - 1200 AD
Technical Explanation: Slit tapestry, which interlocks over 1 warp every 0,5 cm. Sloping lines around the dots
Cross-reference: O.4243, O.4251

Description
The textile consists of 4 panels sewn together. The 3 panels measure 21 cm width-wise and has weft selvages on the two sides – the fourth panel is a fragment 8 cm wide and only with one weft selvage. One of the middle panels also has one warp selvage.

The pattern of the textile is big (20 x 20 cm) jaguars with frayed crowns and "Lambayeque" eyes. Lambayeque is situated north of Pachacamac and flourished between 1000 and 1200 AD The jaguar is often identified with the shaman, and the textile could be from a shaman's mantle (Engelstad, 1984).

Fibre Analysis
The textile has 9 warps and 26 wefts per cm.
Warp: 2 ply Z, 0,4 mm cotton, condition 5.
Weft: 2 ply S, 0,8 mm wool, condition 1.
pH warp, cotton, 6,7.
pH weft, cotton, 6,3.

Acquired by:
From the Gretzer collection. Acquired by the National Museum in 1922 from the Museum für Völkerkunde, Berlin.

Mus. No.: O.4188b
Type: Scarf
Material: Wool, cotton
Technique: Complementary weft weave with substituting colours, plain weave, weft rep
Colour: Red, yellow, brown, black, white
Provenience: Pachacamac
Size: 57 x 59 cm
Date: 1200 – 1450 AD
Cross-reference: O.4151

Description

Square piece with 4 selvages. The textile has horizontal stripes depicting cats and birds woven in complementary weft weave with substituting colours. The pattern is in 3 colours: red in the first shed, and yellow and brown sharing the second shed. The wefts on the front side of the textile always go over 3 or 1 warp. On the back side the red likewise goes over 3 or 1 warp – whereas the brown and yellow wefts are left floating over more warps, according to the pattern.

A brown plain weave is placed in between the 13,5 cm wide pattern stripes, and along one warp selvage is a white weft rep stripe. Around 3 of the selvages are fragments of 7 rows of loop stitch embroidery. The warp is plied from 2 colours : white and brown.

Fibre Analysis

The thread-count is 11 warps and 42 wefts per cm.
Warp: 2 ply Z, cotton, 0,5 mm (tight twist), condition 3.
Weft: 2 ply S, wool, 0,6 mm (loose twist), condition 1.
pH : weft 5,5-6,8.

Acquired by:

From the Gretzer collection. Acquired by the National Museum in 1923 from the Museum für Völkerkunde, Berlin.

Mus. No.: O.4193
Type: Fragment of 3-panelled tunic
Material: Wool
Technique: Supplementary warp and complementary patterning and warp rep plain weave.
Colour: Brown (concealed weft), red, yellow, blue
Provenience: Pachacamac
Size: 97 x 40 cm
Date: 1000 - 1450 AD
Cross-reference: O.4216

Description

The fragment consists of three panels – two identical smaller panels (width 26 cm) arranged at either side of a larger middle panel (46 cm). All three panels have one bottom or top selvage and both side selvages.

The side panels have ca 2 cm wide stripes (with some variation) alternating between plain weave warp rep and complementary warp patterns. These complementary warp patterns are set up with two different colours of warp. The pattern is identical on the two sides of the fabric in opposite colours.

The left panel has a 4 x 4 cm square mending made in a little coarser yarn (0,7 mm) of a little stronger colour than the rest of the weaving.

The middle panel supplementary warp has a figurative warp pattern of two-headed animals and masks. The pattern has 3 different warp colours. It is woven with multiple warps: each shed consists of 6 warp threads – 2 yellow, 2 blue and 2 reds. The colour-bearing units of the pattern are then floated over 3 wefts, where as the other 4 warps (in two different colours) are woven over 1, under 1. The weft is double in this panel. The pattern is only visible on the front side – on the back the warps all pass over 1, under 1 and thus do not create a pattern.

Along the two outer selvages of the side panels are embroidered 3 rows of loop stitches in the same three colours as the weaving.

Fibre Analysis

Warp: 2 ply S, 0,5 mm wool, condition 2.
weft: 2 ply S, 0,8 mm wool (loose twist), condition 2.
pH wool 3,7.

Acquired by:

From the Gretzer collection. Acquired by the National Museum in 1922 from the Museum für Völkerkunde, Berlin.

Mus. No.: O.4195
Type: Fragment
Material: Cotton
Technique: Plain weave (warp rep), painted
Colour: Tan threads, dark brown paint
Provenience: Pachacamac
Size: 75 x 70 cm
Date: 800 – 1200 AD
Technical Explanation: 1. Plain weave warp rep, 2. Positive and negative painting by stencil
Cross-reference: O.4205

Description
Fragment of a 70 cm wide monochrome weaving (part of selvage on both sides) woven in warp rep plain weave.

The textile is decorated with painted stripes of a darker brown, 13 cm wide. The monkey patterns seem to have been made over a stencil: in the dark stripes over a positive monkey form, and in the lighter stripes over a negative, as a reserve paint.

Fibre Analysis
The weaving has 22 warps and 8 wefts per cm.
Warp: 2 ply S, cotton, 0,6 mm, condition 3.
Weft: sg.ply Z, cotton, 0,5 mm, condition 5.
pH warp cotton 5,3.
pH weft cotton 4,8.

Acquired by:
From the Gretzer collection. Acquired by the National Museum in 1922 from the Museum für Völkerkunde, Berlin.

Mus. No.: O.4202
Type: Scarf
Material: Cotton
Technique: Open plain weave, tie-dye
Colour: Tan, brown
Provenience: Pachacamac
Size: 74 x 66 cm
Date: 800 – 1200 AD
Cross-reference: O.D.I.c 267

Description
The textile is sewn together from two pieces (37 x 66 cm each) both with selvages on all sides. After the sewing it has been tied up with little cords in slanting bands along the fabric (where all the light parts of the designs are), and dyed dark brown. The weaving is a very loose plain weave.

Fibre Analysis
The weaving is balanced plain weave and has 5 x 5 threads per cm.
Both warp and weft are sg.ply S, cotton, 0,2-3 mm, condition 2.
pH cotton 6,9.

Acquired by:
From the Gretzer collection. Acquired by the National Museum in 1922 from the Museum für Völkerkunde, Berlin.

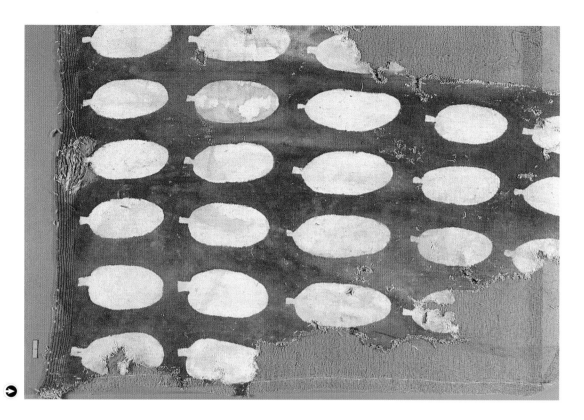

Mus. No.: O.4205.
Type: Fragment
Material: Cotton
Technique: Plain weave 2/2, reserve paint
Colour: White fabric with brown paint
Provenience: Pachacamac
Size: 63 x 46 cm
Date: 800-1200 AD
Cross-reference: O.4195, O.43286

Description

Textile fragment with reserve painted feathers.
The fragment has a bottom/top selvage starting
with thick headings over the first 8 wefts.

Fibre Analysis

11 warps x 9 wefts per cm.
Warp: sg.ply S, cotton, 0,4-0,3mm, condition 3.
Weft: sg.ply S, cotton, 0,4-0,3mm, condition 3.
PH cotton 6,5.

Acquired by:

From the Gretzer collection. Acquired by the
National Museum in 1922 from the Museum für
Völkerkunde, Berlin.

Mus. No.: O.4216
Type: Bag
Material: Wool
Technique: Supplementary warp patterning, warp rep plain weave
Colour: Yellow, brown, red warp and brown concealed weft

Provenience: Pachacamac
Size: 20 cm length, 21,5 cm width
Band: 3,5 x 78 cm
Date: 1400 - 1500 AD
Technical Explanation: Complementary warp patterning. Strap: tube weave with double complimentary pattening
Cross-reference: O.4193

Description

The strap is tube weave with 2 layers of complementary warp interchanged at every patternshift. A double woven complementary warp. The pattern is identical on the two sides in opposite colours.

The bag has stripes of different widths (from 0,5- 2,5 cm) alternating between warp rep plain weave and complementary warp patterning of two colours. The pattern is identical on the two sides in opposite colours.

Fibre Analysis

The band has 32 warps and 5 wefts per cm.
Warp: 2 ply S, wool, 6 mm, condition 3.
Weft: 2 ply S, wool, 6 mm, condition 3.
The bag has 48 warps and 11 wefts per cm.
Warp: 2 ply S, wool, 5 mm, condition 3.
Weft: 2 ply S, wool, 5 mm, condition 3.

Acquired by:

From the Gretzer collection. Acquired by the National Museum in 1922 from the Museum für Völkerkunde, Berlin.

Mus. No.: O.4217
Type: Bag
Material: Wool
Technique: Slit tapestry
Colour: Red, pink, blue, green, brown, black, purple, white
Provenience: Pachacamac (Inca)
Size: 19,5 x 31 cm.
Date: 1450 – 1500 AD
Technical Explanation: Tapestry, loop stitch embroidery
Cross-reference: O.4243, O.4251

Description

The diamond design bag is made in fine tapestry weaving; all the designs have diagonal edges, there are no colour changes parallel to the warp and consequently no need for interlocked joins. It is a typical Inca design. Along the top and sides are 6 rows of loop stitch embroidery, and at the two lower corners two red tassels. A 2 cm fragment of a 1,5 cm wide warp patterned band at the one upper corner is probably left from the carrying band.

Fibre Analysis

The weaving has 10 warps and 52 wefts per cm. The warp is 2 ply S, wool, 0,5mm, condition 5. The weft is 2 ply S wool, 0,5mm, condition 5. pH wool 5,8.

Acquired by:

From the Gretzer collection. Acquired by the National Museum in 1923 from the Museum für Völkerkunde, Berlin.

Mus. No.: O.4223
Type: Band
Material: Wool
Technique: Supplementary warp patterning with spiralling weft (tube weave)
Colour: Brown, yellow, red
Provenience: Pachacamac
Size: 43 x 5 cm
Date: 1000 – 1450 AD
Technical Explanation: Supplementary warp patterning with floating warps at the back between the patterns
Cross-reference: O.4216

Description

The warp is set up in 3 colours. After 1 cm plain weave the warp is divided in two layers, so that the weft can spiral through and create a cylinder shaped weaving.

The pattern-bearing threads are picked up for weaving and left floating loose on the backside of the fabric when not in use – in this case on the inside of the tube.

At the top (the last 6,5 cm of the weaving) the two warp layers are joined into one again, and woven in plain weave with the warps in bundles.

At either end a loop stitch embroidery of three rows covers the top and bottom selvage.

The pattern depicts antropomorphic figures.

Fibre Analysis

The band has 18 warps and 6 wefts per cm.
Warp: 2 ply S, wool, 0,9 mm, condition 3.
Weft: 2 ply S, wool, 0,9 mm, condition 3.
Both have very coarse fibres - 0,06 mm.
pH light wool 3,7.
pH dark wool 4,6.

Acquired by:

From the Gretzer collection. Acquired by the National Museum in 1922 from the Museum für Völkerkunde, Berlin.

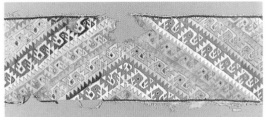

Mus. No.: O.4231
Type: Band
Material: Wool and cotton
Technique: Interlocked tapestry
Colour: 2 browns, white, black, grey/blue, mauve, tan
Provenience: Pachacamac
Size: 68 x 9 cm
Date: 800 - 1500 AD
Cross-reference: O.43316

Description
Very finely woven tapestry band with birds, cats and geometric patterning. All patterns have sloping contours of 5-10 wefts. Most other colours are woven horizontally – except a few excentric wefts.

Fibre Analysis
The band has 16 warps and 60 wefts per cm.
Warp: 3 ply S cotton, 0,3 mm, condition 3.
Weft: 2 ply S wool, 0,3 mm, condition 4.
pH warp cotton 6,7.
pH weft wool 6,8.

Acquired by:
From the Gretzer collection. Acquired by the National Museum in 1922 from the Museum für Völkerkunde, Berlin.

Mus. No.: O.4237
Type: Band
Material: Wool and cotton
Technique: Slit tapestry
Colour: Tan, yellow, white, brown, red, black
Provenience: Pachacamac
Size: 78 x 19 cm
Date: 800 - 1200 AD
Cross-reference: O.4243, O.4251

Description
The tapestry band has a stylised bird motif. All the wefts are horizontal except for the red contours consisting of 3 wefts, which are woven in sloping lines, following the patterns. Along the weft selvages a 0,5 cm wide border is woven – it is interlocked every 0,5 cm with groups of 3 wefts.

Along the weft selvages the band is sewn to a selvage of plain cotton weave of which very little is left.

Fibre Analysis
The tapestry has 8 warps and 44 wefts per cm.
Warp: 3 ply Z cotton, 0,5 mm, condition 2.
Weft: 2 ply S wool, 0,6 mm, condition 1.
The plain weave has 10 x 12 warps /wefts per cm
Warp /weft: 2 ply S cotton, 0,5 mm, condition 3.
pH warp cotton 6,4.
pH weft wool 5,7.

Acquired by:
From the Gretzer collection. Acquired by the National Museum in 1922 from the Museum für Völkerkunde, Berlin.

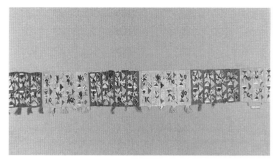

Mus. No.: O.4238
Type: Band
Material: Cotton and wool
Technique: Complementary weft weave with substituting colours
Colour: Red, yellow, white, green, purple, pink
Provenience: Pachacamac
Size: 89 x 12,5 cm
Date: 800 - 1200 AD
Cross-reference: C.N.0. O.41886

Description

The band is pattern-wise divided up in squares of 10-15 cm length. The patterns are alternating between sloping rows of birds in two colours, and vertical rows of birds in many colours.

Where the weaving has sloping pattern-lines the pattern is in two colours: red for the first shed, yellow for the second and so forth. Both wefts go under 1 or 3 warps and likewise over 1 or 3 warps all the time.

Where the weaving has vertical patterns 3 colours are used at a time. Solid red occupies the first shed and always goes under 1 or 3 warps, and over 1 or 3 warps. Two different colours share the other shed, going over 1 or 3 warps on the front-side of the weaving and floating between the pattern units on the back-side.

Fibre Analysis

The thread-count is per cm 10 warps and 30 wefts.
The warp is 3 ply Z, cotton, 0,6 mm, condition 3. The weft is: red: sg.ply Z, 0,4 mm, condition 1, yellow and others: 2 ply S, 0,8 mm, condition 1. pH cotton warp, 6,9.

Acquired by:

From the Gretzer collection, Acquired by the National Museum from the Museum für Völkerkunde, Berlin.

Mus. No.: O.4243
Type: Band
Material: Wool and cotton
Technique: Slit tapestry
Colour: Yellow, green, red, brown, black, white
Provenience: Pachacamac
Size: 69 x 7,5 cm
Date: 800 − 1200 AD
Cross-reference: O.4251, O.4145

Description

Tapestry woven band with weft selvages and cut at the two ends. Along one side the band has every 2 cm over 0,8 cm weft fringes of 1,5 cm's length made by continued wefts.
The patterning of the band is birds.
A lot of the weft has disappeared, but it is impossible to say whether the disappeared weft was all of the same colour.
The band has sloping contours but otherwise horizontal wefts. The vertical slits (at the most 1,5 cm long) are left open.

Fibre Analysis

The weaving has 12 warps and 44 wefts per cm.
Warp: 3 ply Z cotton, 0,4-5 mm, condition 3.
Weft: 2 ply S wool, 0,4 mm, condition 1.
pH warp cotton 5,7.
pH weft wool 5,5.

Acquired by:

From the Gretzer collection. Acquired by the National Museum in 1922 from the Museum für Völkerkunde, Berlin.

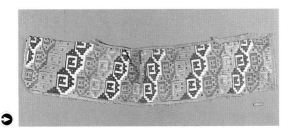

Mus. No.: O.4251
Type: Band
Material: Wool and cotton
Technique: Slit tapestry
Colour: White, brown red yellow, tan
Provenience: Pachacamac
Size: 55 x 12,5 cm
Date: 800 - 1200 AD
Technical Explanation: Slit tapestry with partially floating wefts at the back side,
Cross-reference: O.4145, O.4243

Description

The tapestry woven band is complete with 4 selvages. One weft selvage is in two places 1,5 cm shorter than the rest of the weaving, which must be on purpose in order to shape the band. At one end of this selvage is sewn a 13 cm long, 0,5 cm wide fragment similar to the edge – maybe a similar band.

Along the opposite weft selvage fragments of sewing with a pink thread is left, but none of the material sewn on.

The vertical slits are interlocked over one warp every 0,8-1 mm.

Between the dots 0,5 cm apart the pattern wefts are floated from dot to dot on the back side of the weaving.

The patterning is geometrical designs.

Fibre Analysis

The weaving has 7 warps and 6 wefts per cm.
Warp: 2 ply S cotton, 0,4-6 mm, condition 4.
Weft: 2 ply S wool, 0,5 mm, condition 1
pH warp cotton 5,8.
pH weft wool 6,1.

Acquired by:

From the Gretzer collection. Acquired by the National Museum in 1922 from the Museum für Völkerkunde, Berlin.

Mus. No.: O.4253
Type: Fragment
Material: Cotton
Technique: Discontinuous warp, plain weave
Colour: White, tan, green, blue
Provenience: Pachacamac
Size: 115 x 11 cm
Date: 800 - 1200 AD
Cross-reference: O.10278, O.43336

Description

The weaving was set up with the squares at right angles above each other – each colour in a step pattern (to the right or left) from the former one. The scaffold wefts are gone, and the little squares (in some places attached to the former by one weft and warp in each corner) are sewn together after the weaving was completed. The weaving has 15 warps and 26 wefts per cm, and each square measures 3 x 3 cm.

Fibre Analysis

Warp: cotton, 2 ply S, 0,3 mm, condition 5.
Weft: cotton, 2 ply S, 0,5 mm, condition 5.

Acquired by:

From the Gretzer collection. Acquired by the National Museum from the Museum für Völkerkunde, 1923.

Mus. No.: O.4256
Type: Band
Material: Wool
Technique: Braiding
Colour: Dark brown, light brown
Provenience: Pachacamac
Size: 38 x 3 cm
Date: 800 – 1200 AD
Cross-reference: O.D.I.c 204

Description
The band is braided from 16 strands, arranged with 4 light brown, 4 dark brown, 4 light brown, and 4 dark brown.

Fibre Analysis
The yarn is 2 ply S, wool, 2 mm, condition 1, Each strand is made up of two of these yarns.
pH wool 3,9

Acquired by:
From the Gretzer collection. Acquired by the National Museum in 1923 from the Museum für Völkerkunde, Berlin.

Mus. No.: O.4277b
Type: Tablet
Material: Cotton
Technique: Slit tapestry
Colour: Brown, white, green, light blue, 2 tan
Provenience: Pachacamac (Rimac)
Size: 32 x 32,5 cm
Date: 1100 – 1440 AD
Technical Explanation: Slit tapestry
Cross-reference: O.4131, O.44076

Description
Tapestry with 4 selvages. The design is a (bearded ?) deity with a small monkey-like creature in each hand. He has birds in his crown and two more bearded persons and two more monkeys are on either side of him. A line of lama-like animals is underneath the god, and the panel is framed by a row of double serpents.
The tapestry has sloping contours – otherwise the weft is horizontal.

Fibre Analysis
The weaving has 8 warps and 36 wefts per cm. The warp is 3 ply S cotton, 0,5 mm, condition 3. The weft is sg.ply Z cotton, 0,3 mm, condition 2.
pH cotton 6,6.

Acquired by:
From the Gretzer collection. Acquired by the National Museum in 1922 from the Museum für Völkerkunde, Berlin.

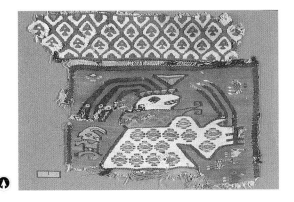

Mus. No.: O.4277c
Type: Fragment
Material: wool and cotton
Technique: Slit tapestry
Colour: Red, pink, yellow, brown, blue, 2 greens, lavender
Provenience: Pachacamac
Size: 15 x 20 cm
Date: 800 - 1200 AD
Cross-reference: O.4243, O.4251

Description

Fragment of an amazing piece of tapestry depicting 5 small rodents and a priest or deity with snake hair. Above is a 4 cm wide border with spade designs. The longer (over 1 cm) vertical slits in the hands and along the border are sewn together after weaving.

Another piece of the same weaving is in Ethnologisches Museum, Berlin VA 568 a-c.

Fibre Analysis

The weaving has 11 warps and 60 wefts per cm.
Warp 3 ply Z cotton, 0,5 mm, condition 2.
Weft 2 ply S wool, 0,3-4 mm, condition 1.
pH warp cotton 6,7.
pH weft wool 4,8.

Acquired by:

From the Gretzer collection. Acquired by the National Museum in 1922 from the Museum für Völkerkunde, Berlin.

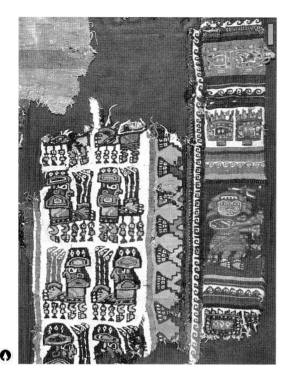

Mus. No.: O.4281c
Type: Fragment
Material: Wool, cotton
Technique: Slit and dovetailed tapestry
Colour: White, green, blue, red, pink, yellow, lavender, brown, black
Provenience: Pachacamac (Lambayeque)
Size: 43 x 29 cm
Date: 800 – 1200 AD
Cross-reference: O.4277c, O.42776

Description

Fragment of a very fine tapestry with ornamental and anthropomorphic designs. The long vertical slits are dovetailed over one warp every 0,5-1 cm. The weft is mostly horizontal with few exceptions.

Another part of this same weaving is on exhibit in Ethnologisches Museum, Berlin
(VA 57793a-c.)

Fibre Analysis

The weaving has 9 warps and 30 wefts per cm. The warp is 2 ply S, cotton, 0,4 mm, condition 3. The weft is sg.ply Z and 2 ply S wool, 0,8 mm, condition 1.
pH warp cotton, 6,8.
pH cartboard, 6,2.

Acquired by:

From the Gretzer collection. Acquired by the National Museum in 1922 from the Museum für Völkerkunde, Berlin.

Mus. No.: O.4284
Type: Tapestry woven pieces for application.
Material: Wool and cotton
Technique: Slit tapestry
Colour: Red, pink, lavender, 2 blues, 2 yellows, 3 greens, tan, brown, black, white
Provenience: Pachacamac
Size: Smallest 13 x 8 cm, biggest 61 x 20 cm
Date: 1100 - 1400 AD
Technical Explanation: Slit tapestry, fringes, tassels, loop weave
Cross-reference: O.4137

Description

Various little tapestry woven pieces for application on cotton material. No. 4 has a little plain weave material attached to it.
The curbed crowns are warps woven a few cm and left with the rest of the warp loose as an uncut fringe. It is then curbed and sewn on to the tapestry.
No. 8 seems to be the lower edge of no 7.
No. 1 and 2 also have loop weave and tassels.
Anthromorphic figures and animals wear huge cresent head ornaments.

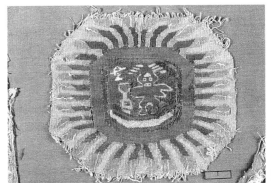

Fibre Analysis

No. 7 has per cm 9 warps and 40 wefts.
Warp: 2 ply Z, cotton, 0,5 mm, condition 2.
Weft: 2 ply S wool 0,5 mm, condition 1.
pH warp cotton 5,8.
pH weft wool 5,9.
No. 5 has per cm 10 warps and 16-26 wefts.
Warp: 2 ply Z cotton, 0,4 mm, condition 2.
Weft: 2 ply S wool, 0,6-1 mm, condition 1.
No. 8 like no 7.

Acquired by:

From the Gretzer collection. Acquired by the
National Museum in 1923 from the Museum für
Völkerkunde, Berlin.

Mus. No.: O.4288a
Type: Fragment
Material: Cotton
Technique: Double weaving with single face brocading
Colour: White, brown
Provenience: Pachacamac
Size: 41 x 17 cm
Date: 800 – 1200 AD
Cross-reference: O.4155

Description
Fragment of a very fine double weaving with a pattern of birds, snakes, cats and brocaded human faces. The textile is sewn together from two pieces along their side selvages.

Fibre Analysis
The weaving has 12 wefts and 18 warps per cm.
Warp: sg.ply, S cotton, 0,4 mm, condition 5.
Weft: 2 ply, S cotton 0,6 mm, condition 4.
Brocade: 2 ply, S wool 1,2 mm, condition 1.
Sewing: sg.ply, S cotton 0,3 mm, condition 5.
pH dark cotton 7,3.
pH light cotton 7,0.

Acquired by: as O.4288b

Mus. No.: O.4288b
Type: Fragment
Material: Cotton
Technique: Double weaving
Colour: White, brown
Provenience: Pachacamac
Size: 23 x 12 cm
Date: 800 – 1200 AD
Cross-reference: O.4155

Description
A small fragment of a very fine double weaving with two- headed birds, geometrical figures, meandering bands and strange 2- legged animals. The textile has two selvages at an angle (top/ bottom and side) and two thick headings (1,2 mm).

Fibre Analysis
The weaving has 12 wefts and 20 warps per cm.
Warp: sg.ply, S, cotton, 0,3 mm, condition 5.
Weft: sg.ply, S, cotton, 0,4 mm, condition 3.
pH dark cotton 6,1.
pH light cotton 6,3.

Acquired by:
From the Gretzer collection. Acquired by the National Museum in 1922 from the Museum für Völkerkunde, Berlin.

Mus. No.: O.4288c
Type: Cutting from larger cloth.
Material: Cotton
Technique: Partial supplementary warp patterning and discontinous warp.
Colour: White, brown
Provenience: Pachacamac
Size: 19,5 x 20 cm
Date: 800 - 1200 AD
Cross-reference: O.43336, O.4373

Description

The textile has one top/ bottom selvage and two side selvages. It is a part of a weaving sewn together from various bands, which are made from brown and white squares woven in discontinuous warp. Every other square is also patterned with a bird – and geometrical motifs in supplementary warp weaving. The supplementary warps (the white ones) are only partial, i.e. they are only set up on 19 cm lengthwise (like in discontinuous warp). The supplementary warps are woven in

warp rep plain weave, where they are visible from the front, and left floating on the back where not, leaving the brown warps here to be woven in a more balanced plain weave.

The remaining part of this weaving, from which this square was cut, is still in Ethnologisches Museum, Berlin VA 20092 (consisting of 27 similar squares in discontinous warp with or without pattering.

Fibre Analysis

The weaving has 11 wefts per cm, and in the stripes 32 warps per cm, and in the brown parts 16 warps per cm.
Warp: 2plyS, cotton, 0,4 mm, condition 4.
Weft: 2plyS, cotton, 0,4mm, condition 4.
pH cotton 6,8.

Acquired by:

From the Gretzer collection. Acquired by the National Museum in 1922 from the Museum für Völkerkunde, Berlin.

Mus. No.: O.4294a
Type: Fragment
Material: Cotton
Technique: Plain weave and painting
Colour: White fabric with brown paint
Provenience: Pachacamac (Chimu)
Size: 43 x 15 cm
Date: 1100 - 1450 AD
Cross-reference: O.4294c, O.4295

Description
Fragment probably from a border of a textile painted with various meandering fish and bird designs.

Fibre Analysis
There are 13 warps and 10 wefts per cm. The fragment is woven in plain weaving (2 warps, 1 weft).
Both warp and weft are sg.ply S, cotton, 0,3 mm, condition 4.
pH light cotton 6,8.
pH dark cotton 6,3.

Acquired by:
From the Gretzer collection. Acquired by the National Museum in 1922 from the Museum für Völkerkunde, Berlin.

Mus. No.: O.4294c
Type: Fragment
Material: Cotton
Technique: Plain weave and print
Colour: White, dark brown paint
Provenience: Pachacamac (Chimu)
Size: 33 x 45 cm
Date: 1100 - 1450 AD
Cross-reference: O.4294, O.4295

Description
The textile fragment is without selvages, and thus hard to tell warp from weft, but probably has 2 warps per 1 weft. The design seems to have been printed on, as it is very accurate and small in the lines. Is consists of anthromorphic figures carryind staffs or spears and 2-headed animals.

Fibre Analysis
The weaving has 24 warps, and 15 wefts per cm.
Both warp and weft are sg.ply S, cotton, 0,2–3 mm, condition 4.
PH cotton 6,8.

Acquired by:
From the Gretzer collection. Acquired by the National Museum in 1922 from the Museum für Völkerkunde, Berlin.

Mus. No.: O.4298
Type: Fragment
Material: Cotton
Technique: Single face brocade
Colour: Brown foundation, white, tan, blue patterning
Provenience: Pachacamac
Size: 62 x 48 cm
Date: 800 - 1200 AD
Cross-reference: O.4299, O.4170

Description
Fragmented textile with one weft selvage. Decorated by single face brocade, where the wefts are laid in between the two warp layers and cover the warp in the front completely. The pattern is flying birds around a diamond with meandering patterns with a monkey-like animal in the middle.

Fibre Analysis
The weaving has per cm 18 warps and 14 wefts.
Warp: 2 ply S, cotton, 0,3-5 mm, condition 5.
Weft: 2 ply S, cotton, 0,3-5 mm condition 5.
Pattern weft: sg.ply Z, cotton, 0,5 mm, condition 3.
pH plain weave cotton 6,8.

Acquired by:
From the Gretzer collection. Acquired by the National Museum in 1923 from the Museum für Völkerkunde, Berlin.

Mus. No.: O.4295
Type: Fragment
Material: Cotton
Technique: Plain weave and painting
Colour: White, 3 browns, black
Provenience: Pachacamac (Chimu)
Size: 36 x 41 cm
Date: 1100 - 1450 AD
Technical Explanation: Plain weave, painting and reserve painting
Cross-reference: O.4294a+c

Description
Textile fragment painted with stripes, reserve painted dots in the stripes and little men with cresent headgear. The foundation material is plain woven (2 warps, 1 weft) cotton.

Fibre Analysis
The threadcount is 12 warps and 9 wefts per cm.
2 warp/ 1 weft plain weave.
Warp: sg.ply S, cotton, 0,5 mm, condition 4.
Weft: sg.ply S, cotton, 0,4 mm, condition 3.
pH dark cotton 5,4.
pH light cotton 6,0.

Acquired by:
From the Gretzer collection. Acquired by the National Museum in 1923 from the Museum für Völkerkunde, Berlin.

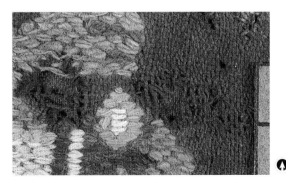

Mus. No.: O.4299b
Type: Fragment
Material: Cotton and wool
Technique: Single face and two face brocade
Colour: Tan foundation; yellow and red patterning
Provenience: Pachacamac
Size: 40 x 43 cm
Date: 1100 - 1450 AD
Cross-reference: O.4298, O.4170

Description

A plain weave cotton fabric with a big (30 x 30 cm) "jaguar-duck" brocaded repeatedly upwards. The pattern threads go under 1 warp, and over 4 warps in the first shed. In the second shed the warp in the middle of the previous shed is picked up. The feet of the animal are in two face brocade, the pattern wefts floating on the back side of the fabric between the claws of the animal.

The fragment has one weft selvage.

Fibre Analysis

The thread-count is per cm 20 warps and 10 wefts.
Warp and weft: 2 ply S cotton 0,3-5 mm, condition 5.
Pattern weft : 2 ply S wool, 0,6-8 mm, condition 3.
pH plain weave cotton 5,8.

Acquired by:

From the Gretzer collection. Acquired by the National Museum in 1923 from the Museum für Völkerkunde, Berlin.

Mus. No.: O.4301a
Type: Fragment
Material: Wool
Technique: Complementary warp patterning.

Colour: Brown (concealed weft) yellow, blue, red warp
Provenience: Pachacamac.
Size: 41 x 63 cm
Date: 1000 - 1450 AD
Cross-reference: C.N.0, O.4151, O.4238

Description

63 cm of a panel with 3 selvages – one bottom or top and two side selvages. The warp is set up in stripes of two colours – red/ yellow alternating with red/blue. The pattern is identical at the other side in opposite colours. The pattern could be lobsters.

Another fragment of the same textile is in Ethnologisches Museum, Berlin.

Fibre Analysis

The weaving has 22 warps and 6 wefts per cm.
Warp: 2 ply S, 0,8 mm (loose twist) wool, condition 1.
Weft: 2 ply S, 1 mm (loose twist) wool, condition 1.
Both have very coarse fibres – 0,06 mm.
pH warp wool 5,8.
pH weft wool 5,3.

Acquired by:

From the Gretzer collection. Acquired by theNational Museum in 1922 from the Museum für Völkerkunde, Berlin.

Mus. No.: O.4311a
Type: Fragment
Material: Wool, cotton
Technique: Slit and dovetailed tapestry
Colour: Yellow, black, pink, blue, red, green, lavender, white
Provenience: Pachacamac
Size: 40 x 13,5 cm
Date: 800 - 1200 AD
Cross-reference: O.4311b

Description

The tapestry woven band has selvage on 3 sides. Along one weft selvage there is fragment of a sewing to a cotton material. The pattern weft is horizontal, only the contours of 2-3 wefts lining out the patterns are woven in sloping lines. Along the sides are vertical slits interlocked over one warp every 0,5 cm.

Fibre Analysis

The weaving has 13 warps and 34 wefts per cm. The warp is 3 ply Z cotton, 0,4 mm, condition 3. The weft is 2 ply S wool, 0,6-7 mm, condition 1. pH wool 5,7. pH cartboard 6,5.

Acquired by:

From the Gretzer collection. Acquired by the National Museum in 1922 from the Museum für Völkerkunde, Berlin.

Mus. No.: O.4311b
Type: Fragment
Material: Wool and cotton
Technique: Slit tapestry
Colour: Yellow, red, lavender, pink, green, brown, black, white, blue
Provenience: Pachacamac
Size: 31 x 45 cm
Date: 800 - 1200 AD
Technical Explanation: 1. Slit tapestry, 2. Loop stitch embroidery
Cross-reference: O.4311a, O.43256
2. p.

Description

Fragment of a textile consisting of two panels. One panel – 43 cm wide – has two weft selvages and one warp selvage. The other panel is only a small cut-off fragment 2 cm wide, with weft selvage along the edge sewn to the first panel. The small fragment does not continue the pattern of the first panel but whether it is the same pattern just staggered from each other is impossible to say.

The warp selvages have fragments of loop stitch embroidery.

The weft of the black contours is gone in most of the weaving, leaving little holes in the packed weft, where the warp can be seen.

The design shows monkeys carrying triangles (?).

Fibre Analysis

The weaving has 8 warps and 48 wefts per cm. The warp is 3 ply Z cotton, 0,6 mm, condition 5. The weft is 2 ply S wool, 0,8 mm, condition 3. pH warp, cotton, 5,7.

Acquired by:

From the Gretzer collection. Acquired by the National Museum in 1922 from the Museum für Völkerkunde, Berlin.

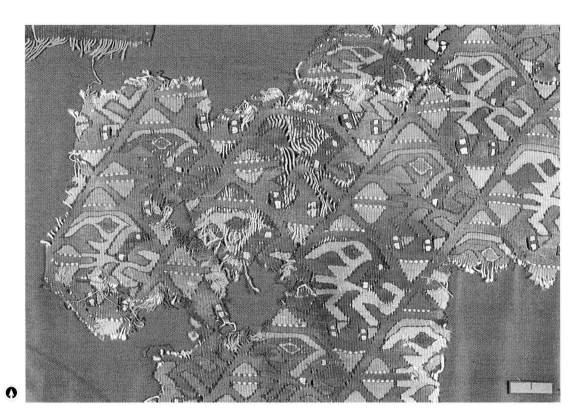

Mus. No.: O.4325b
Type: Fragment
Material: Wool and cotton
Technique: Slit tapestry
Colour: Tan, brown, yellow, red, white
Provenience: Pachacamac
Size: 26 x 30 cm
Date: 800 - 1200 AD
Cross-reference: O.4311b

Description

The tapestry woven piece has one weft selvage along which there are traces of sewing (to another material, which no longer exists).

It has vertical wrap-around contours and sloping contours woven with 3-4 wefts. There is some non horizontal weft patterning.

The motif is monkeys carrying triangles (?) in their hands.

Fibre Analysis

The weaving has 10 warps and 32 wefts per cm.
Warp: 3 ply Z cotton, 0,6 mm, condition 1.
Weft: red and yellow: 2 ply S wool, 0,4 mm, condition 1 tan: sg.ply S cotton, 0,4 mm, condition 1.
pH warp cotton 6,6.
pH weft red wool 5,7.

Acquired by:

From the Gretzer collection. Acquired by the National Museum in 1923 from the Museum für Völkerkunde, Berlin.

Mus. No.: O.4325c
Type: Fragment
Material: Wool, cotton.
Technique: Slit and dovetailed tapestry, shaped warp, complementary weft weave with substituting colors.
Colour: Pink, yellow, black, white, lavender, green, curry

Provenience: Pachacamac
Size: 18 x 24 cm
Date: 800 - 1200 AD
Cross-reference: O.43256, O.4311

Description

The textile has selvages on all sides. It is set up and woven as a normal warp; but the weft is only interwoven according to the stepped shape. After completing the weaving the non woven warps are cut and sewn down into the weaving.

The textile has at the bottom a folded 1 cm wide band woven in complementary weft weave with substituting colours.

After this edge the fabric is woven in slit tapestry, where the vertical contours are wrapped around one warp. The slits – when longer than 2 cm – are dovetailed around one warp.

The fabric is probably for application at the corner of a cotton tunic.

The design shows birds and stylized animals.

Fibre Analysis

The weaving has 10 warps and 40 wefts per cm. The warp is 2 ply S, cotton, 0,4-5 mm, condition 2.

The weft is 2 ply S, wool, 0,4-5 mm, condition 1. pH cotton 6,7.

Acquired by:

From the Gretzer collection. Acquired by the National Museum in 1922 from the Museum für Völkerkunde, Berlin.

Mus. No.: O.4228c
Type: Fragment
Material: Cotton and wool
Technique: Tapestry, discontinous warp, plain weave
Colour: Brown/red/white/yellow
Provenience: Pachacamac
Size: 12 x 56 cm
Date: Ca. 800 – 1200 AD
Cross-reference: O.43316, O.4369

Description

A fragment of a tapestry woven band, which may be the border of a tunic. A little piece of plain woven cotton material is left sewn on to the straight side of the band, and sewing thread along the side is also present – and implies that the band was sewn to a piece of plain weave cotton fabric similar to what is often seen in tunics.

The pattern in the tapestry is a row of feathers. The top of the feathers is shaped using the discontinuous warp technique.

Fibre Analysis

The tapestry weaving has 9 warps and 16 wefts per cm.
The warp is 2 ply S, cotton, 0,6 mm, condition 1.
The weft is 2 ply S, wool, 0,4 mm, condition 1.
The sewing thread is 2 ply S wool.
The fabric that the tapestry band has been sewn to is a plain weave (14 x 14 per cm) of 2 ply S, cotton, condition 5.

Acquired by:

From the Gretzer collection. Acquired by the National Museum in 1922 from the Museum für Völkerkunde, Berlin.

Mus. No.: O.4331b
Type: Fragment of a tunic
Material: Wool
Technique: Interlocked tapestry
Colour: 2 yellow, brown, red, white, black
Provenience: Pachacamac (Wari)
Size: 55 x 47 cm
Date: 1200 - 1400 AD
Cross-reference: O.4231

Description
The textile fragment consists of two panels sewn together along the only pieces of selvage existing. The design differs much from other Pachacamac textiles both in technique (interlocked tapestry), material (both warp and weft are wool) and in colours (predominantly red, yellow, black and white). The piece is probably Wari.

The weaving has interlocks of every 3. weft alternating with every weft. In some places it has open slits, which are sewn together.

The fabric is from a tunic and the joining of the two panels is vertical down the side of the garment. The warp direction is therefore horizontal when worn. The warp in this kind of tunics is as wide as from the bottom of the tunic, over the shoulder and to the other bottom side – these Wari tunics being quite long this makes a warp almost 2 m wide. It can be concluded that this tunic was woven on an upright loom, because it was not possible to weave on a backstrap loom.

The design shows bats. The major part of the tunic (with neck slit) is in Ethnologisches museum, Berlin (VA53062).

Fibre Analysis
The thread count is 13 warps and 40 wefts per cm. Warp: and weft are both 2 ply S, wool, 0,4 mm, condition 3.
pH wool 5,7.

Acquired by:
as O.4328b

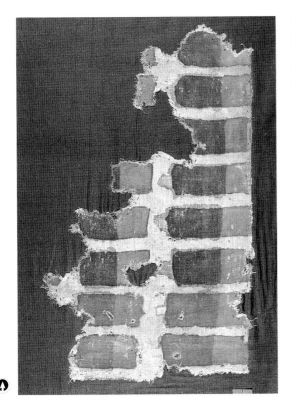

Mus. No.: O.4328b
Type: Fragment
Material: Cotton
Technique: Plain weave (2/2) and painting.
Colour: White fabric with blue and two brown paints
Provenience: Pachacamac
Size: 18 x 22 cm
Date: 800 - 1200 AD
Cross-reference: O.4205, O.4369, O.4231

Description
The plain woven fabric is woven with two warps and two wefts in each shed.

The decoration is 2-coloured feathers. When painting the feathers one blue and one brown colour are used – the dark brown is the blue and the brown on top of each other.

Between the feathers the textile is painted tan.

Fibre Analysis
The weaving has 11 wefts and 20 warps per cm.

Both the warp and the weft are sg.ply S, cotton, 0,3 mm, condition 2.

pH cotton 4.

Acquired by:
From the Gretzer collection. Acquired by the National Museum in 1922 from the Museum für Völkerkunde, Berlin.

Mus. No.: O.4333b
Type: Fragment
Material: Cotton
Technique: Plain weave 2/1 – discontinous warp
Colour: Blue, tan, white, green.
Provenience: Pachacamac (Chimu)
Size: 53 x 43 cm.
Date: 1100 – 1450 AD
Cross-reference: O.4253, O.10278

Description

The textile consists of five 10 cm wide bands
sewn together lengthways. Each band consists of
many small step-fret shaped textiles – each one
woven individually and sewn together. These
shaped warps are set up on a scaffold weft frame,
and the scaffold wefts pulled out after the weaving
is completed, thus making the pieces fall apart.
The weaving is a 2 warps/1 weft plain weave.

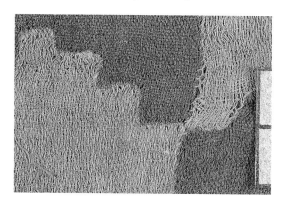

Fibre Analysis

The weaving has 14 warps and 15 wefts per cm.
The warps are double yarns.
Both warp and weft are sg.ply S cotton, 0,1 mm,
condition 3.
pH cotton 6,9.
Surface pH 6.

Acquired by:

From the Gretzer collection. Acquired by the
National Museum in 1922 from the Museum für
Völkerkunde, Berlin.

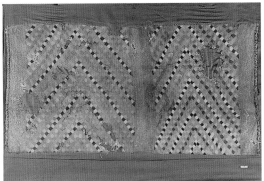

Mus. No.: O.4335
Type: Fragment
Material: Wool, cotton
Technique: Interlocked tapestry
Colour: Red, yellow, pink, brown, black, white
Provenience: Pachacamac
Size: 41 x 46 cm
Date: 1400 - 1550 AD
Cross-reference: O.4337

Description

Textile patterned with squares of 1 x 1 cm. Along the top and/or bottom selvages are solid brown and red weft stripes. The textile consists of two panels (23 x 46 cm and 18 x 34 cm) sewn together with red wool along the red stripes.

The entire white weft is gone, leaving the former white squares with just the warp left. Along the remaining selvage are 4 rows of loop stitches. The textile has sharp cuts – probably from the grave robbers looting the mummies.

Fibre Analysis

10 warps x 28 wefts per cm.
Warp: 3 ply Z, cotton, 0,5mm, condition 1.
Weft: 2 ply S, wool, 0,4mm, condition 3-5.

Acquired by:

From the Gretzer collection. Acquired by the National Museum in 1923 from the the Museum für Völkerkunde, Berlin.

Mus. No.: O.4337
Type: Cloth
Material: Cotton and wool.
Technique: Complementary weft weave and tapestry.
Colour: Black, tan, brown, red.
Provenience: Pachacamac.
Size: 69 x 35 cm
Date: 1400 - 1550 AD
Cross-reference: O.4335, C.N.0.

Description

The weaving is complete with 4 selvages. Along the two end selvages are 3 rows of loop stitches. The tapestry pattern is squares, woven on the edge like diamonds of an average of 0,7 cm.

The complementary weft pattern is big and small triangular faces, woven in relief effect in one colour.

The textile seems to have been washed, and the colours have run.

Along both side selvages are fragments of plain weave cotton material.

Fibre Analysis

Tapestry: 10 warps x 26 wefts per cm.
Complementary weft: 10 warps x 28 wefts per cm.
Warp: 3 ply S, cotton, 0,7mm, condition 3.
Weft: 2 ply S, wool, 0,5mm, condition 3.

Acquired by:

From the Gretzer collection. Acquired by the National Museum in 1923 from the Museum für Völkerkunde, Berlin.

Mus. No.: O.4340a
Type: Fragment
Material: Cotton, wool
Technique: Plain weave with two faced lancé brocading
Colour: White, brown, blue.
Provenience: Pachacamac
Size: 48 x 32 cm
Date: 800 - 1200 AD
Cross-reference: O.3032

Description

A plain-woven fragment with two face selvage-to-selvage brocading. The pattern is arranged so that the patterning is identical on both sides but in alternate colours (white/ brown) and in that way reminds of a true double weaving.

The textile has one selvage left and along this a little fragment of a blue woollen fabric sewn to the brocaded textile.

Fibre Analysis

The brocaded fragment has 10 wefts and 17 warps per cm (the warps are double).
Brown weft: sg.ply Z, cotton, 0,4 -0,8 mm, condition 3.
White weft: sg.ply Z, cotton, 0,2 mm, condition 3.
White warp: sg.ply S, cotton, o,5 mm, condition 3.
Blue added fabric:
Warp: 2 ply S loose twist, wool, 0,8 mm, condition 4.
Weft: sg.ply S, cotton, 0,5 mm, condition 5.
Thread: 2 ply S, cotton, 0,5 mm, condition 5.
pH cotton 6,9.

Acquired by:

From the Gretzer collection. Acquired by the National Museum in 1922 from the Museum für Völkerkunde, Berlin.

Mus. No.: O.4346
Type: Fragment
Material: Wool and cotton
Technique: Gauze weave, plain weave and tapestry
Colour: Tan gauze, reds, yellow, green, black and blue
Provenience: Pachacamac
Size: 40 x 54 cm.
Date: 800 - 1200 AD
Cross-reference: O.D.I.c 230

Description

A 10 cm wide tapestry woven band with a geometrical pattern is sewn to a gauze woven net.

The net holes are 5 – 8 mm, and around each 15 cm a narrow stripe of balanced plain weave breaks the gauze woven net structure horizontally and vertically and makes the textile appear chequered. The net material is sg.ply, S cotton.

The tapestry band has a white-tan cotton warp and multicoloured woollen weft. The patterns are all geometrical and have slanted lines. Many of the patterns have a narrow, black, woven contour around.

Fibre Analysis

The tapestry has 11 warps and 23 wefts per cm.
Tapestry warp: 3 ply Z, cotton, 0,5 mm, condition 3.
Tapestry weft: 2 ply S, wool, 0,5 mm, condition 3.
Net: warp: sg.ply S, cotton, 0,4 mm, condition 3.
Weft: sg.ply Z, cotton, 0,25 mm, condition 2.
pH net cotton 7,0.
pH tapestry warp cotton 7,0.
pH tapestry weft wool 5,4.

Acquired by:

From the Gretzer collection. Acquired by the National Museum in 1922 from the Museum für Völkerkunde, Berlin.

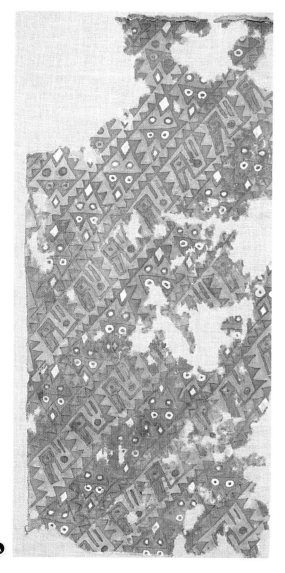

Mus. No.: O.4349
Type: Fragment
Material: Cotton.
Technique: Painted plain weave fabric
Colour: White foundation with 3 different brown paints

Provenience: Pachacamac
Size: 108 x 50 cm
Date: 800 – 1400 AD
Technical Explanation: 1. Plain weave,
2. Fringe
Cross-reference: O.4352

Description

The fragment has some selvage left along one long and one short side. Along one long selvage are traces of stitching thread for sewing the fabric to another fabric. Along the short selvage is a fringe made from a double yarn Z, 2 S, 4 Z. This yarn is wound around a very degraded cotton cord still left inside the fringe. Chain stitches are sewn along the stick holding all the spiral loops in place. The fringe is 0,5 cm and sewn on to the fabric.

The painted pattern shows birds and geometrical figures.

Fibre Analysis

The plain weave has 14 x 10 threads per cm.
The fabric warp is sg.ply S, cotton, 0,5 mm, condition 3.
The fabric weft is 2 ply S, cotton, 0,5 mm, condition 3.
The fringe material is 2 ply S, cotton, 0,5 mm, condition 1.
The chain stitch are 2 x 2 ply S, cotton, 0,5 mm, condition 3.
The sewing thread is 2 ply S, cotton, 0,5 mm, condition 1.
The inner fringe material is cotton, condition 3.
pH light cotton 7,0.
pH dark cotton 6,7.
pH inner fringe cotton 5,4.

Acquired by:

From the Gretzer collection. Acquired by the National Museum in 1922 from the Museum für Völkerkunde, Berlin.

Mus. No.: O.4352
Type: Fragment
Material: Cotton
Technique: Plain weave with painting
Colour: White, brown
Provenience: Pachacamac
Size: 54 x 53 cm
Date: 800 – 1200 AD
Cross-reference: O.4349

Description

Fragment of a plain-woven textile with one (bottom or top) selvage with three thick headings.

At one selvage fragments of little threads are tied to the textile with 3-8 cm between. Maybe it was used for attaching tassels or little metal plates at the bottom of this may-be-tunic.

The painted decoration is a pattern of geometrical figures and birds.

Fibre Analysis

32 warps x 16 wefts per cm.
Warp: sg.ply S, cotton, 0,2 mm, condition 4.
Weft: sg.ply S, cotton, 0,3 mm, condition 4.
pH cotton dark 6,3.
pH cotton light 6,6.

Acquired by:

From the Grezer collection. Acquired by the National Museum in 1922 from the Museum für Völkerkunde, Berlin.

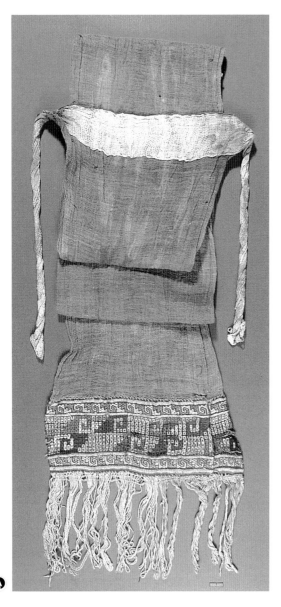

Mus. No.: O.4355
Type: Breechcloth
Material: Cotton and wool
Technique: Plain weave, supplementary weft weave with substituting colours, fringe
Colour: Plain weave: tan
Tapestry: white, red, yellow green, tan, pink
Provenience: Surroundings of Lima
Size: 202 x 31 cm. Belt: 101 x 6 cm
Date: 1100 – 1400 AD
Cross-reference: O.4151, O.41886

Description

Breechcloth in plain weave with 10,5 cm wide tapestry woven band and 15 cm wide fringe.

The ornamented piece has 4 selvages; it has narrow weft rep horizontal stripes and meandering bands at the top and bottom framing a much used square dot pattern, all in suplementary weft weave in 3 or more colours.

The top and bottom meandering border has a brown weft in every second shed, and a red and yellow sharing the other shed. The brown weft always goes over 1 or 3 warps on both sides of the fabric, where as the red/yellow goes over 1 or 3 on the front side but is left floating from pattern unit to pattern unit on the back side.

The middle part (the dot pattern) has a dark brown weft in every second shed; the other sheds are shared by 2 colours (with floating back-wefts) at a time – but these two colours are altered along the warp as in tapestry weave. The coloured wefts also shift horizontally on the backside of the weaving floating to new patterns higher up on the weaving.

At the opposite end of the breechcloth a 6 x 102 cm plain woven band is in the middle sewn on to the breechcloth edge. The two ends of this band are left on either side of the breechcloth for tying.

Fibre Analysis

Plain weave:
The thread-count per cm is 9 warps, 15 wefts.
Warp and weft are sg.ply S cotton, 0,3-5 mm, condition 1.
Tapestry:
per cm 7 warps, 36 wefts.
Warp: 2 ply S, cotton, 0,3 mm, condition 5.
Weft: 2 ply S wool, 0,8mm, condition 1.
Fringe: 2 ply S wool, 1,5 mm, condition 1.
pH: plain weave cotton 4,7; tapestry warp cotton 4,7; fringe wool 5,6.

Acquired by:

From the Gretzer collection. Acquired by the National Museum in 1923 from the Museum für Völkerkunde, Berlin.

Mus. No.: O.4364
Type: Band and tassel
Material: Wool
Technique: Tapestry, loop pile, tassels, discontinuous warp
Colour: Tan, brown, red, pink, blue, mauve
Provenience: Ancon
Size: 50 x15 cm
Date: 1100 – 1400 AD
Cross-reference: O.4139

Description

A 4,5 cm wide tapestry band woven with vertical non sewn slits. The band alternates between 5 cm solid brown with a diamond pattern in the middle, and 5 cm of 3 one cm wide bands set 0,5cm apart. To cover these slits 4 warpthreads are added for the solid squares and finished off again after each square. The narrow bands have 2 stripes each with 3 rows of loop pile 2-3 mm high with 3-4 wefts between.

In each diamond is a big tassel consisting of 12 little tassels.

In each loop pile are attached two smaller tassels. Each tassel is 2-3,5 cm long.

Fibre Analysis

8 warps x 18 wefts per cm.
Warp: 2 ply S, wool, 0,5mm, condition 1.
Weft: 2 ply S, wool, 0,5mm, condition 1.
Tassels: 2 ply S, wool, 0,5mm, condition 3.
pH wool 6,1.

Acquired by:

From the Gretzer collection. Acquired by the National Museum in 1922 from the Museum für Völkerkunde, Berlin.

Mus. No.: O.4366
Type: Band with fringe
Material: Cotton
Technique: Slit tapestry
Colour: Yellow, white, black, red, orange, tan
Provenience: Ancon
Size: 15 x 23 cm
Date: 1000 – 1200 AD
Cross-reference: O.4284, O.4251

Description

The 8 cm wide band is woven in slit tapestry. The vertical contours are wrapped around one warp and the slits are left open (at the most 1,5 cm long). The little bearded men resembling Santa Claus is a much used design.

Above and beneath the little men are weft rep stripes. The fragment has 3 selvages (2 warp – one weft) and is cut at one side. Probably the fragment was a bottom border from a tunic. At the top are traces of sewing – although no material is left.

The fringe (7 cm) is the weft with 2 warps interwoven at the top to hold the weft fringe in place.

Fibre Analysis

The thread-count is 9 warps by 56 wefts per cm.
Warp: 2 ply Z cotton, 0,6 mm, condition 3.
Weft: 2 ply S cotton, 0,4 mm, condition 3.
2 ply S wool, 0,5 mm, condition 3.
Fringe: 2 ply S wool, 0,7 mm, condition 3.
pH wool 5,7.

Acquired by:

From the Gretzer collection. Acquired by the National Museum in 1923 from the Museum für Völkerkunde, Berlin.

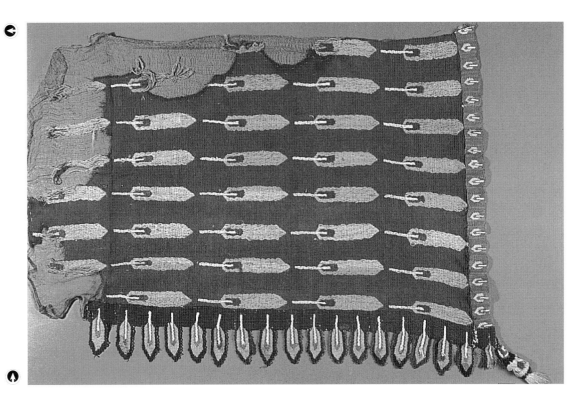

Mus. No.: O.4369
Type: Fragment
Material: Wool, cotton
Technique: Discontinuous warp, tapestry, single face brocade, tassels
Colour: Brown, yellow, red
Provenience: Marquez
Size: 59 x 43 cm.
Date: 1100 – 1450 AD
Cross-reference: O.4328c, 0,43286

Description

A plain woven textile with feather imitations in 3 different techniques. The textile has one side- and one bottom selvage.

The middle piece is plain woven (2 warp, 1 weft) cotton material with a single face brocade pattern of feathers.

At the side is a tapestry woven band, 2,2 cm wide, also with a pattern of feathers.

At the bottom is another tapestry woven band set up partially in discontinuous warp, making the feathers stick out from the band.

The textile has a tassel in the corner where the selvages meet, made by small tassels spiralled around a core.

Fibre Analysis

Middle cloth: 17 wefts x 20 warps (double) per cm.
Warp: sg.ply,S, cotton, 0,2 mm, condition 5.
Weft: sg.ply S, cotton, 0,2 mm, condition 3.
Pattern weft: 2 ply S, wool, 0,6 mm, condition 1.
Tapestry band: 52 wefts x 10 warps per cm.
Warp: 2 ply S, cotton, 0,6 mm, condition 3.
Weft: 2 ply S, wool, 0,5 mm, condition 1.
Bottom band: 16 wefts x 7 warps per cm.
Warp: 2 ply Z, cotton, 0,6 mm, condition 3.
Weft: 2 ply S, wool, 0,6 mm, condition 1.
Sewing thread: sg.ply Z, cotton, 0,3 mm, condition 3.
Tassel, 2 ply S, wool, 0,6 mm, condition 1.
pH red wool 3,6.
pH cotton 5,7.

Acquired by:

From the Gretzer collection and Acquired by the National Museum in 1923 from the Museum für Völkerkunde, Berlin.

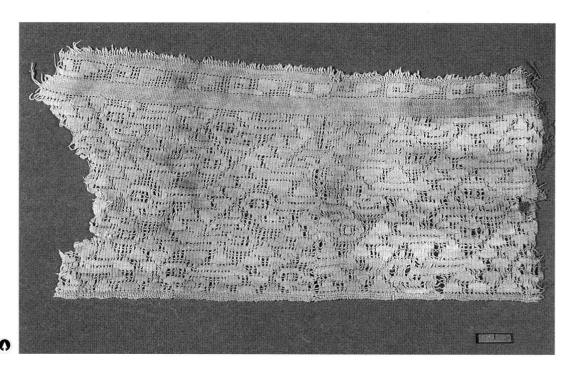

Mus. No.: O.4372
Type: Fragment
Material: Cotton
Technique: Gauze weaving and brocade
Colour: Cream
Provenience: Chancay
Size: 30 x 15 cm
Date: 1000 - 1400 AD
Cross-reference: O.D.I.c 230

Description

The textile fragment consists of two pieces of individually woven brocaded gauze weavings, sewn together. One of the long sides has a selvage. From the selvage edge is woven: 2 rows of plain weave (1 warp, 2 weft), then 6 mm balanced plain weave, 11 cm brocaded gauze, 1 cm balanced plain weave, 1 cm brocaded gauze, 0,5 cm plain weave.

The technique is simple gauze weave, where the same two warp threads are twisted around each other with each input of the weft.

The weft reps brocading has 2 twisted warp threads in each shed, and 5 wefts for each gauze weave weft. There is 10 warps and 3 wefts per cm in the gauze. The pattern show triangles and little birds.

Fibre Analysis

The thread counts are:
Plain weave: 12 x 9 per cm.
Gauze: 12 x 4 per cm.
Brocade: 3 pattern wefts per foundation weft.
The yarns are all 2 ply S, cotton, 0,4 mm, condition 3.
pH cotton 7,3.

Acquired by:

From the Gretzer collection. Acquired by the National Museum in 1922 from the Museum für Völkerkunde, Berlin.

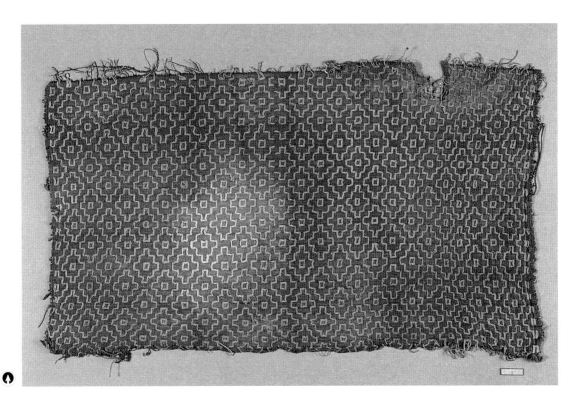

Mus. No.: O.4373
Type: Fragment
Material: Cotton
Technique: Plain weave, supplementary warp and weft
Colour: Brown foundation, white patterning
Provenience: Chancay
Size: 45 x 25 cm.
Date: 1000 - 1400 AD
Cross-reference: O.4288c

Description

The fragment is a patterned plain weave which has selvage along the top and the bottom and along one side, the other side is cut off.

Alternating two rounds of brown threads one round of tan thread set up the warp. Only the brown warps are woven in the plain weave – the tan warps are pulled through the warp after each 4 wefts, so they alternately show up on the front of the textile and on the back.

At the same time a similar supplementary weft consisting of two tan threads are at each 4th weft row pulled through the fabric, over 8 warps, under 8. The patterning can be compared to horizontal and vertical running stitch embroidery, but in this case the patterning is done during the weaving with supplementary warps and wefts.

Fibre Analysis

The thread count is 14 warps and 9 wefts per cm. All the threads used are 2 ply S, cotton, 0,3-4 mm.
Condition: warp 2, weft 5, pattern 3, sewing 3.
pH weft cotton 6,0.
pH pattern warp cotton 6,4.

Acquired by:

From the Gretzer collection. Acquired by the National Museum in 1922 from the Museum für Völkerkunde, Berlin.

Mus. No.: O.4374
Type: Fragment
Material: Cotton.
Technique: Plain weave, painting.
Colour: White and 3 different browns
Provenience: Chancay
Size: 153 x 60 cm
Date: 1000 - 1400 AD
Cross-reference: O.4142, O.4195

Description

The fragment is a coarse, plain weave fabric made from loosely and irregularly spun cotton fibres. Only one of the long sides has selvage. The pattern outlines have been marked with a 0,5 cm dark brown line and then the colours have been filled in between the markings.

The design shows anthropomorphic, feline and geometrical figures.

Fibre Analysis

The plain weave has 14 x 6 threads per cm. Both warp and weft are 2 ply S, cotton, 0,8-1 mm, condition 3.
pH cotton 6,8.

Acquired by:

From the Gretzer collection. Acquired by the National Museum in 1922 from the Museum für Völkerkund, Berlin.

Mus. No.: O.4399
Type: Tunic
Material: Cotton and wool
Technique: Warp faced plain weave and double faced brocade
Colour: Tan foundation, yellow, red, black patterning
Provenience: Ica.
Size: 91 x 77 cm
Date: 1400 - 1550 AD
Cross-reference: O.5674, O.4170

Description

The tunic is a very fine warp faced plain weave (warp rep) in cotton, with double brocaded woollen patterns at the chest and the back, and 9 brocaded stripes at the lower end of the tunic. The brocading is inlaid as a weft rep consisting of 8 warps from the plain weave in each shed. The brocading is done with a red and a black weft simultaneously, so the red goes over and the black goes under the same 8 warps. Thus the pattern comes out identical – red on one side, where it is black on the other.

The design of each pattern square is two stylised birds.

The shape of the tunic is Inca inspired – longer than it is wide. It is woven in two pieces with the warp vertical and sewn together mid front and at the sides, leaving a 34 cm slit for the neck and 32 cm slits for the arms.

Fibre Analysis

The plain weave has 46 warps and 15 wefts per cm.
Warp and weft are 2 ply S, cotton, 0,3 mm, condition 3.
Pattern weft: 2 ply S, wool, 0,6 mm, condition 1.

Acquired by:

From the Gretzer collection. Acquired by the National Museum in 1923 from the Museum für Völkerkunde, Berlin.

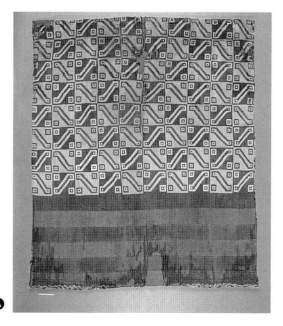

Mus. No.: O.4400
Type: Tunic
Material: Wool
Technique: Tapestry
Colour: Brown, red, yellow
Provenience: Pachacamac (Inca)
Size: 75 x 164 cm
Date: 1400 - 1550 AD
Cross-reference: O.4399, 0.4281c

Description

The tunic is woven on an upright loom with the wefts going from the front bottom of the tunic, over the shoulder and to the back bottom. The technique is interlocked tapestry, and the design is called the Inca key. It is a *Qompi* weaving. A standardised weaving for official use, with the embroidered zigzag at the bottom indicating that it is a royal tunic. Several similar tunics in different colours exist in various museums in the Western World as seen in Rowe, A.P. "Provincial Inca Tunics of the South Coast of Peru", Textile Museum Journal, 1992.

The neck slit is made by inserting a scaffold weft and warping the two shoulder-parts separately, like in discontinuous warp.

The squares are 7 x 7 cm.

Fibre Analysis

9 warps x 40 wefts per cm.
Warp and weft: 2 ply S, wool, condition 3.

Acquired by:

From the Gretzer collection. Acquired by the National Museum in 1923 from the Museum für Völkerkunde, Berlin.

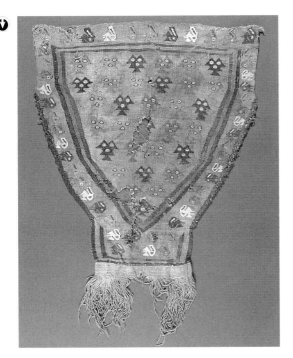

Mus. No.: O.4405
Type: Breechcloth
Material: Wool/cotton
Technique: Tapestry
Colour: Yellow, red, white.
Provenience: Unknown provenience, Peru
Size: 50 x 36 cm
Date: 800 - 1450 AD
Technical Explanation: Tapestry, shaped warp, weft fringe
Cross-reference: O.4284, O.44076

Description

The weaving is started with a width of 36 cm. After 12 cm the side warps are gradually left non woven until the weaving measures 32 cm lengthwise and is 16,5 cm wide. This narrow width is woven straight for 6 cm. A weft fringe, with 2 cm weaving and 10 cm loose hanging wefts, is sewn to the narrow end of the textile. After weaving the warps there is – along the sloping sides – woven an edge band 1,2 cm wide, which is bent to the back of the weaving. The warps are cut and used to sew the edge band down. The weaving has 8 warps and 13-16 wefts per cm. The long slits in the tapestry are sewn together after the weaving is completed. The design is pelicans along the edges and probably sting-ray on the middle part.

Fibre Analysis

Warp: cotton, 3 ply Z, 0,6 mm, condition 1.
Weft: wool, 2 ply S, 0,6-1 mm, condition 3.

Acquired by: as O.4400

Mus. No.: O.4407b
Type: Tablet (fragment)
Material: Cotton
Technique: Tapestry, interlocked and dovetailed
Colour: Brown, 2 tan, white, blue
Provenience: Unknown (Rimac)
Size: 25 x 27 cm
Date: 1100 - 1440 AD
Cross-reference: O.42776

Description

Fragment of a probably square tapestry piece, which has been appliquéd to a plain weave cotton material.

The pattern depicts 3 warriors with spears in their hands and a fourth floating in the air above them holding his ear. Maybe a shaman.

In some places the tapestry wefts are interlocked, in some places dovetailed.

Fibre Analysis

Tapestry: 12 warps and 44 wefts per cm.
Warp: 2 ply S, cotton, 0,2-3 mm, condition 3.
Weft: sg.ply Z, cotton, 0,3-8 mm, condition 3.
Plain weave: 12 warps and 18 wefts per cm.
Warp and weft: 2 ply S, cotton, 0,6 mm, condition 3.
pH cotton 6,0.

Acquired by:

From the Gretzer collection. Acquired by the National Museum in 1923 as a donation from Dr. Aage Schmidt.

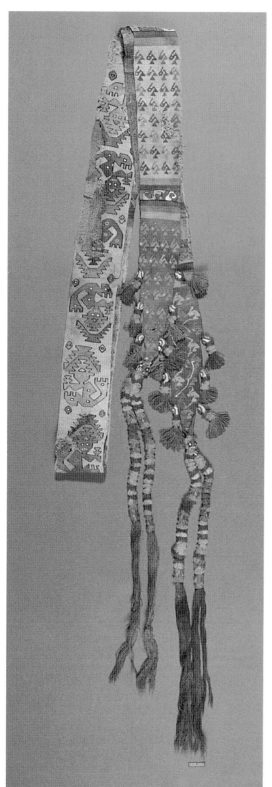

Mus. No.: O.5199
Type: Woven band
Material: Wool/cotton.
Technique: Tapestry woven band with shaped ends and tassels.
Colour: Blue, red, yellow, green, black, brown and white
Provenience: Chanchan (Chimu).
Size: 3 m x 6,5 cm
Date: 1300 – 1400 AD
Cross-reference: O.4364, O.4366

Description

A heavy foundation cord is tied around the centre of each group of yarns that will form the tassel. Then the yarns are folded down and the tops wound with another yarn.

The band is woven in tapestry, the middle part with black outlines around each figure. The motifs are birds at the ends, geometric designs and a monkey like animal in the middle. The two ends of the belt are narrowed in by placing 6 of the outer warps on both sides of the belt in the tassels each 3,5 cm. The furred cords are constructed by stringing tassels one on top of the other. There are two 18 cm tassel-cords at each end of the band and each again ends with a 20 cm long loose hanging tassel.

Fibre Analysis

The thread count is 9 warps x 60 wefts per cm.
Warp: 2 ply S, cotton, 0,5 mm, condition 4.
Weft and fringes: 2 ply S, wool, 0,5-0,8 mm, condition 3.
pH red wool 6,0.

Acquired by:

General Castonier donated the belt to the National Museum in 1926. He had received it as a present by Major Otto Holstein in Trujillo. According to a letter from Otto Holstein the belt is from the ruins of Chanchan (The capital of the Chimu culture, 3-4 miles north of Trujillo).

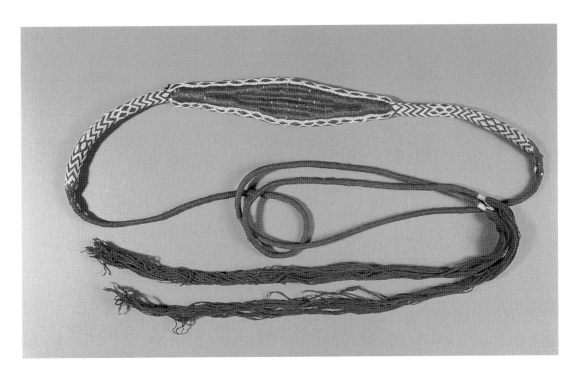

Mus. No.: O.5659
Type: Sling
Material: Wool, cotton
Technique: Cord wrapping, braiding
Colour: Red, yellow
Provenience: Peru
Size: 285 x 1 - 7 cm
Date: Unknown
Cross-reference: O.4032

Description

The middle part of the sling is a flat oval shaped piece, 23 cm long, 8 cm wide at the middle interwoven over thick cotton foundation cords. There is a 5 cm slit in the middle, and the edges are decorated with stem stitch embroidery. The foundation yarns are gathered and a cotton cord wrapped tightly around them, and stem stitch embroidery is made over 16 cm on either side of the flat middle piece. The foundation cord is reduced and 65 cm braiding of 1 cm diametrically, is made in each end of the sling. 5o cm fringe of loose hanging braiding wool finishes the sling at either end.

Fibre Analysis

The woollen yarns used are 2-ply S, 1,7 mm, condition 1.
pH wool 5,0.
Surface pH 4,7.

Acquired by:

Collected by Edmond Haüflein during his long stay in Lima. Bought by the National Museum in 1922. No provenience stated.

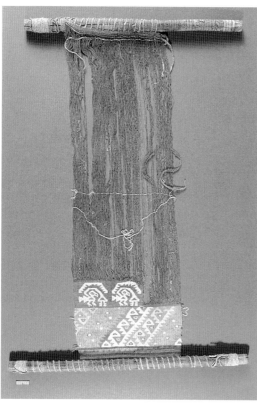

Description

The loom is probably a "test-loom", used for trying out and later for copying the patterns.

The warp is cotton. It is attached to the end sticks by a helping cord, so the weaving can be woven with selvages at both ends. The cross-tie is still in the warp, but no shed sticks. The top beam is decorated with brown stripes and circles.

The weaving is decorated with birds and geometric patterns.

Many warp threads are broken and new ones reattached with weaver's knots.

Fibre Analysis

The textile has 10 warps and 26 wefts per cm.
Warp: 2 ply S, cotton, 0,2 and 0,5mm, condition 3.
Weft: 2 ply S, wool, 0,4mm, condition 1.

Acquired by:

Collected by Edmond Häuflein who lived several years in Lima. Acquired by the National Museum in 1922. No provenience stated.

Mus. No.: O.5660
Type: Test-loom
Material: Wool, cotton, wood
Technique: Tapestry
Colour: White, yellow, red, brown
Provenience: Unknown
Size: 48 x 16 cm
Date: 1200 - 1400 AD
Cross-reference: O.4325c, O.4284

Mus. No.: O.5668
Type: Fragment
Material: Wool
Technique: Slit tapestry
Colour: Red, black, yellow, white, blue
Provenience: (Wari)
Size: 30 x 17 cm
Date: 800 – 1200 AD
Cross-reference: O.4282

Description
The fragment is ornamented with birds and stylised or geometric patterns. It could be provincial Wari, as the patterns are repeating themselves in different dimensions, like on other Wari tunics. Also the material (pure wool) is a Wari sign, and the stylised figures.

Fibre Analysis
The textile has 7 warps and 28 wefts per cm. Warp and weft: 2 ply S, wool, 0,7mm, condition 3.

Acquired by:
Collected by Edmond Häuflein, who lived several years in Lima. Acquired by the National Museum in 1922. No provenience stated.

Mus. No.: O.5674
Type: Fragment
Material: Cotton and wool
Technique: Double face brocade
Colour: Brown foundation, yellow and red patterning
Provenience: Ica
Size: 24,5 x 9 cm
Date: 1400 – 1550 AD
Cross-reference: O.4399

Description

Fragment of a double face brocaded textile with a bird motif. The pattern is identical on the back side of the textile. The pattern wefts go under 4 over 4 warps crossing the two sheds of the plain weave.

The design shows typical provincial Inca influence.

Fibre Analysis

The weaving has 16 warps and 11 wefts per cm.
Warp: 2 ply S, cotton, 0,5 mm, condition 3.
Weft: sg.ply S, cotton, 0,5 mm, condition 3.
Pattern weft: 2 ply S, wool, 0,8 mm, condition 1.
pH plain weave cotton, 5,1.

Acquired by:

From Edmond Haüflein's Peru collection. Acquired by the National Museum in 1923.

Mus. No.: O.5677
Type: Front piece of a headband
Material: Wool
Technique: Tapestry
Colour: White, brown, red, yellow, black
Provenience: Unknown
Size: 21 x 4 cm
Date: 1400 – 1550 AD
Cross-reference: O.4311b, O.4325c

Description

The little textile is complete with selvages on all sides. It has 14 cm of 4 cm wide weaving and 4 woven fringes (1 x 7 cm). The end selvage at the fringe end is woven like little loops.

The piece is probably an end piece of a headband, which has been sewn to a longer band for wrapping around the head.

The "E.T."-like figure suggests that it could be a Chachapoyas weaving.

Fibre analysis

10 warps x 28 wefts per cm.
Warp: sg.ply Z, wool, 0,3 mm, condition 3.
Weft: 2 ply S, wool, 0,7 mm, condition 3.

Acquired by:

Collected by Edmond Häuflein, who spent several years in Lima. Acquired by the National Museum in 1922. No provenience stated.

Mus. No.: O.5678
Type: Fragment
Material: Wool and cotton
Technique: Plain weave and stem stitch embroidery
Colour: White, green, blue, red, yellow, black, ochre
Provenience: Paracas
Size: 24 x 13 cm
Date: 200 BC - 200 AD
Cross-reference: O.8525

Description
Fragment of an embroidered mantle or tunic. The foundation cloth is of red, plain weave cotton material (13 x 13 threads per cm). The embroidery is in wool and done in stem stitch technique (over 4 under 2 threads). All imaginable colours are used. The motive is a "flying" person (shaman) holding a string of beans in one hand and a sword with trophy heads in the other. Other beans and root vegetables are attached to him and an extra trophy head is hanging from his back. At his front he is wearing a typical Paracas ornament.

Fibre Analysis
Plain weave: 2 ply S, cotton, 0,4 mm, condition 5.
Embroidery: 2 ply S, wool, 0,3 mm, condition 1.

Acquired by:
Collected by Edmond Häuflein who lived several years in Lima. Acquired by the National Museum in 1922. No provenience stated.

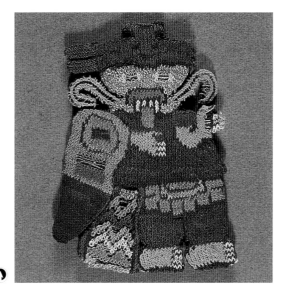

Mus. No.: H.6345
Type: Fragment probably from a fringe of a mantle
Material: Wool and cotton
Technique: Loop stitch
Colour: Green, yellow, beige, red, black, olive green
Provenience: Paracas
Size: 6,3 x 4,6 cm
Date: 200 BC - 200 AD
Cross-reference: U.N.1

Description

The fragment is a little man with a head dress much represented in the textiles of Paracas. He is sticking out his tongue and has serpent-like lines coiling out from each side of his neck. He seems to be carrying a zigzag patterned bag at his belt and a large one on his shoulder. The figure is 3 dimensional, and identical on the two sides. He is made in woollen loop stitch on a knotted, brown foundation of cotton material. The pink of his face is made from two yarns twisted together from a white and a red coloured yarn. He is sewn starting from the top of his head.

Fibre Analysis

The threads are cotton 2 ply S; 0,15 mm, condition 5. and wool 0,2 mm, condition 5.
The inner looping is 2 ply S, cotton, 0,15 mm, condition 5.
pH wool 3,8.

Acquired by:

Donated by Knud Biehl in 1984. A colleague in Pisco gave the textile to him in the beginning of the 1950s.

Mus. No.: O.5678
Type: Fragment
Material: Wool and cotton
Technique: Plain weave and embroidery.
Colour: White, red, blue, yellow, brown, grey, pink, black
Provenience: Paracas
Size: 38 x 30 cm
Date: 200 BC - 200 AD
Cross-reference: O.5678

Description

Fragment of a mantle, breechcloth or tunic with 9 stem stitch embroidered figures (9x5 cm) holding double axes and trophy heads in their hands. They are all wearing the typical Paracas front plate. They have trophy heads at their ankles and different animals depicted on their chests, and snakes sliding out of their armpits.

The textile has been impregnated with a substance which has by now glassified and made the textile very crisp. It is not reversible. This impregnation must have been done before the textile was acquired by the museum, as a piece of the same textile is likewise impregnated kept in Ethnologisches Museum, Berlin to were it came from the same collektor.

Fibre Analysis

Cotton: 2 ply S, 0,4 mm, condition 5.
Wool: 2 ply S, 0,3 mm, condition 5.

Acquired by:

From Guillermo Schmidt-Pizarro's collection. Acquired by the National Museum in 1938.

Mus. No.: O 6712
Type: Triangular mantle.
Material: Cotton and feathers
Technique: Plain weave and feather mosaic
Colour: Tan foundation;
Feathers: yellow, black, green/turqoise, orange
light blue.

Provenience: Pachacamac, Lurin (Tiahuanaco).
Size: 130 x 70 cm.
Date: 800 - 1200 AD
Technical Explanation: Feather mosaic
Cross-reference: O.6790, O.6789

Description

The fragment is a balanced plain woven fabric –
originally a square piece measuring 105 x 105 cm
and folded in a triangle. The feathers are sewn
through both layers of the fabric. The feathers are
sewn on, in rows following the desired patterns.
Very little of the feathers are left but it is possible
to see from the stitching, that the design has been
a winged person or a butterfly in the middle with
a 20 cm wide outer edge band of stripes and
meandering designs.

The feather design is only intact on a small piece
of the border.

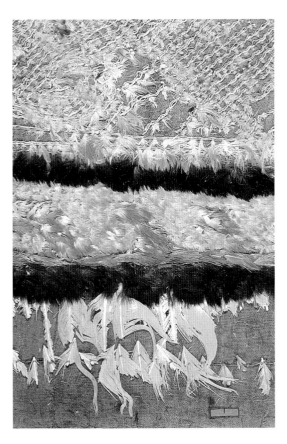

Fibre Analysis

The weaving is balanced plain weave, 10 x 10
threads per cm.
Both warp and weft are sg.ply S, cotton, 0,2 mm,
condition 3.
pH cotton 5,7.
pH feather 6,6.

Acquired by:

From Gretzer's collection in Hannover. Given to
the National Museum in 1927 by Dr. phil. Aage
Schmidt, with the marking on its box:
    "Pachacamac (Tiahuanaco), Federumhänge von
Lurin".

Mus. No.: O.6789
Type: Tunic (fragment)
Material: Cotton foundation, feather decoration.
Technique: Warp rep plain weave, feathers sewn on
Colour: Tan foundation, feathers: yellow, red, blue
Provenience: Unknown
Size: 86 x 84 cm
Date: Unknown
Technical Explanation: Feather mosaic
Cross-reference: O.6712, O.6790

Description
One side of a feather tunic. The foundation is woven in warp rep plain weave (1 warp, 2 weft), and consists of 2 panels sewn together mid front.

The fabric is covered with horizontal rows (1 cm between them) of feathers, each set with 0,6 mm between them. From the top 10 cm wide bands of red feathers are alternating with 3-5 cm wide yellow feather bands. At the bottom is a 22 cm blue feather band.

Fibre Analysis
6 warps and 5 wefts per cm.
Warp: 2 ply S, cotton, 0,7 -1 mm, condition 3.
Weft: 2 ply S, cotton, 0,7 -1 mm, condition 1.
Sewing thread: 4 ply Z, cotton, condition 3.
pH cotton 4,7.
pH feather 6,0.

Acquired by:
From Edmond Haüflein's collection. Donated to the National Museum in 1929 by Knud Rasmussen and others.

Mus. No.: O.6790
Type: Tunic (fragment)
Material: Cotton foundation, feather decoration.
Technique: Feathers sewn on to the fabric
Colour: Tan foundation material, feathers: yellow, orange, turqoise
Provenience: Unknown
Size: 63 x 70 cm
Date: Unknown
Technical Explanation: Feather-mosaic
Cross-reference: O.6712, O.6789

Description
The fragment is almost one complete side of a 2 panel tunic. It has a 18 cm long slit for the neck opening, which is further cut to 34 cm. The tunic has selvages at both sides. It is woven in balanced plain weave with 8 x 8 threads per cm. The yellow and orange feathers (3-5 cm long) are sewn on to the woven fabric in horizontal rows with 1 cm between the rows. The narrow orange stripe has the feathers sewn on vertically along the vertically slanting lines.

The turquoise feathers, which are much smaller than the yellow and orange feathers (hard to measure their original size because they are so deteriorated) are sewn on in horizontal rows with only 0,5 cm between the rows.

Fibre Analysis
The plain woven foundation is balanced and has 8 x 8 threads per cm.
The warp is sg.ply S, cotton, 0,5 mm, condition 5.
The wefts is 2 ply S, cotton, 0,5 mm, condition 5.
The sewing thread is 2 ply S, cotton, 0,5 mm, condition 4.
pH cotton 5,9.
pH feathers 4,8.

Acquired by:
From Edmond Haüflein's collection. Donated to the National Museum by Knud Rasmussen and others in 1929.

Mus. No.: O.6999 a, b, c
Type: Fragments of a mantle
Material: Woollen embroidery on cotton foundation
Technique: Stem stitch embroidery on plain woven cotton
Colour: Blue plain weave with black, yellow, olive, red, green, blue and white embroidery
Provenience: Paracas
Size: Each piece 8 x 14,5 cm
Date: 200 BC - 200 AD
Cross-reference: O.5678, O.8525

Description

A double headed eagle with woollen threads in stem stitch technique is embroidered on the balanced plain weave cotton foundation textile. One stitch per thread. The fragment is one of 89 embroidered double headed eagles from the middle part of a Paracas mantle. Around the middle was an edge of 22 embroidered larger double headed eagles (15 x 26-30 cm). The eagles on the middle part were crosswise alternating rows of 5 red eagles and 5 green/ red/black/ yellow/ olive green eagles. Around the edge the eagles were black, yellow and olive green, so that every second was green and the two other colours alternating in between. The museum has 3 of the little eagles – a yellow, an olive green and a black.

Fibre Analysis

Both the cotton weaving yarns and the woollen embroidery yarns are 2-ply S, wool, 0,3 mm, condition 1.
Cotton, 2 ply S, 0,4, condition 3.

Acquired by:

The three fragments were given to the museum in 1933 by Heinrich Hardt (Berlin), who had a large collection of Peruvian archaeological textiles. Mr. Hardt cut the three pieces off the original Paracas mantle and sent them as a souvenir of a pleasant morning meeting to the director of The Ethnographical Department, National Museum, Thomas Thomsen. Mr. Hardt also sent a drawing of the original mantle with colour indications, so it must be supposed that he cut the fragments off a complete mantle!

Two big fragments of the same mantle are in Völkerkunde Museum in Munich (1/2) and Ethnologisches Museum in Berlin (1/4).

Mus. No.: O.10267
Type: Bag
Material: Wool, cotton
Technique: (Top to bottom): braiding, twining, looping, plain weave, tapestry weave, looping, flat double wrapping, fringe and tassels
Colour: Beige, yellow, red, black, white
Provenience: Probably Nazca
Size: 44 x 10-19 cm

Date: 0 – 600 AD
Technical Explanation: Flat double wrap
Cross-reference: O.4030, O.10268

Description

The bag itself is of 2 ply S non dyed cotton (1 mm) and woven in 1 warp/ 2 weft plain weave. The plain weave measures 6 cm lengthwise. Then continues a 9 cm long tapestry weave which has 3 of the plain weave warps in each shed. The weft is 2 ply S wool.

At the top of the bag, is 3 cm looped net, (simple looping) by a coarse cotton yarn, which ends in 2,5 cm twisted yarns. The net is finished by a braided edge in coarse brown wool.

Under the bag is by 1 cm simple looping net attached a 10 cm long flat double stem-stitch wrapped textile. The stem-stitches are made from two 2 ply S wool yarns, that are Z twined together. The thread count is 5 stitches per cm.

At each corner of the bag is a woollen tassel with a cord wrapped stem-stitched top part.

At the bottom of this textile is sewn a 14 cm long fringe (2 ply S, 1,5 mm) made by the same yarn as the stem-stitches.

Fibre Analysis
Wool, condition 1.
Cotton, condition 4.
pH wool 6,3.
pH cotton 7,1.

Acquired by:
Donated to the National Museum by Marie Nielsen in 1959. Collected by her brother who lived in Peru. No provenience stated.

Colour: Natural beige, brown, red and yellow
Provenience: Probably Nasca
Size: 18 -10 x 48 cm
Date: 0 – 600 AD
Cross-reference: O.4030, O.10257

Description
The top edge of the bag is braided in dark brown wool, then comes a 3 cm wide piece of twisted cotton from a thick cotton yarn. The same yarn is used in the 2,5 cm wide looped part. This looping is commenced from below, attached to the woven material of the bag, and continued into the twining (6 ply Z, 2 mm).

The bag itself is of 6 cm balanced plain weave (8 x 8 per cm), warp: sg.ply S, weft: two threads of sg.ply S cotton, the lower part is 7 cm tapestry weave, where each shed consists of 4 warp threads.

Underneath the bag is 10 cm cord wrapping (2 ply S, 1 mm), and under this an 18 cm fringe sewn to the cord wrapping part. The fringe consists of twisted threads (2-ply S twined – like the cord wrapping thread) and is uncut at the end.

Fibre Analysis
Condition: cotton 3, wool 1.
pH plain weave cotton 6,5.
pH fringe wool 5,6.
Surface pH cotton 4,8.
Surface pH wool 5,1.

Acquired by:
Donated to the National Museum in 1959 by Maria Nielsen, who had it from her brother in Peru. No provenience stated.

Mus. No.: O.10268
Type: Bag
Material: Cotton and wool
Technique: Top part: Simple looping
The rest: plain weave, tapestry, cord wrapping, fringes

Mus. No.: O.1O.271
Type: Tassel
Material: Wool, cotton wrapping
Technique: Cord wrapping
Colour: Red, yellow and white. The stuffing yarn is green wool
Provenience: Maybe Nasca
Size: The pattern wrap: 5 cm diameter, 8 cm long
The fringe measures 20 cm
Date: If Nasca, 0 - 600 AD
Cross-reference: O.D.I.c 229, O.10277

Description
Around a foundation bundle of yarn, a heavy cotton yarn is wound in a close spiral, with as much distance as required for each embroidery stitch. A stem stitch embroidery is made between these wrapping cords in the desired pattern. In this case with a 2-ply S twist yarn. The embroidery is made with two such threads alongside each other.

Fibre Analysis
Cotton, sg.ply Z, 0,3 mm, condition 1.
Wool, 2 ply S, 1,3 mm, condition 1.

Acquired by:
Donated to the National Museum in 1959 by Maria Nielsen, who had it from her brother in Peru. No provenience stated.

Mus. No.: O.10277
Type: Furred cord ending in a tassel
Material: Wool and cotton.
Technique: "Simili velour"
Colour: Red, yellow, black
Provenience: Peru (Nasca)
Size: 5 cm diameter, 18 cm long
Date: 0 - 600 AD
Cross-reference: O.D.I.c 229, O.10271

Description
The cord is made as a square-knot net in cotton with wool of different colours inserted in each knot. The wool piles are cut afterwards. The net is made over a thick cotton foundation cord. At the end a red woollen tassel.

Fibre Analysis
Pile: wool non spun, condition 1.
Net: cotton, 2 ply S, 0,4 mm, condition 5.
pH cotton 5,2.
pH wool 5,7.

Acquired by:
Donated to the National Museum in 1959 by Maria Nielsen, who had it from her brother in Peru. No provenience stated.

Mus. No.: O.10278
Type: Tunic
Material: Wool, cotton
Technique: Discontinuous warp
Colour: Red, yellow, blue, white
Provenience: Southern coast of Peru
Size: 63 x 75 cm
Date: 600 - 900 AD
Cross-reference: O.4253

Description

Piece of a tunic (no selvages) in discontinuous warp. The foundation warp/weft is red wool and the warp pattern is yellow, blue and white wool with a brown cotton weft. The wefts in the patterns are only half as many as in the foundation cloth. The pattern weft is tied between the foundation sheds ca 2 cm away from the pattern – a new weft is inserted for every step in the pattern. The foundation weft turns from the pattern without interlocking or dovetailing, but the pattern weft is stitched to the foundation a few mm from the selvage. So the pattern weft must have been inserted after the foundation weft was woven. The white pattern warps have almost disappeared.

Fibre Analysis

Foundation thread count is 24 warps and 9 wefts per cm.
Warp: 2 ply S, wool, 0,5 mm, condition 3.
Weft: 2 ply S, wool, 0,5 mm, condition 3.
Pattern thread count is 24 warps and 4 wefts per cm.
Warp: 2 ply S, wool, 0,5 mm condition 3.
Weft: 2 ply S, wool, 0,4 mm, condition 3.
pH wool 5,8.

Acquired by:

Donated to the National Museum in 1959 by Maria Nielsen, who had it from her brother in Peru. No provenience stated.

Mus. No.: O.10319
Type: Fragment
Material: Wool
Technique: Sprang
Colour: Tan
Provenience: According to collector: Nasca
Size: 134 x 44 cm
Date: 0 - 600 AD
Cross-reference: none

Description

The textile is made in the sprang technique, which is an interlinking technique, where threads the width of the textile are stretched on a frame. The threads are then interlinked around the middle, and you get two symmetrical halves – one on either side of the working place. In the middle of a sprang textile a securing thread will be placed, to keep both halves in place. This securing thread can be seen in the photo. If this thread is removed the whole textile will fall apart. The threads can after the work is finished be secured by sewing along the middle line, and then cut in two halves, and then the evidence of the technical procedure is lost.

Fibre Analysis

The textile consists of 138 threads in all, resulting in an approximately 3 threads per cm (varying, as the textile is with a changing pattern).
The yarn is 2 ply S, wool, 0,6 mm, condition 5
pH wool 3,2.
Surface pH 3,4.

Acquired by:

Found in 1959 close to Nasca; Donated the National Museum by Dan Sadolin, who brought it in Peru.

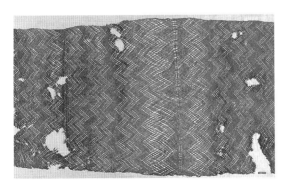

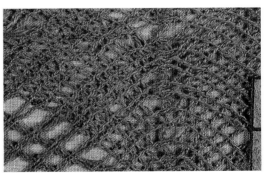

Mus. No.: C.N.6
Type: Four-pointed-hat
Material: Cotton
Technique: Double weave
Colour: White/ brown
Provenience: Nasca
Size: 47 cm diameter, 8 cm tall, top square: 7 x 7 cm
Date: 0-600 AD
Cross-reference: O.4155

Description

Double woven hat, consisting of: one piece of 47 (warp length) x 8 cm (weft width) sewn together to a cylinder, and a top square (7 x 7 cm) sewn to the top in the middle of the cylinder, so that the side panel folds in 3 cm in each corner. To this corner fold is sewn a 2 cm long tuft of many strands of Z twined cotton threads with a little red tassel of non spun red cotton fibres tucked in at the top. At the bottom edge of the hat is sewn a yellow woollen yarn.

Fibre Analysis

The weaving has 11 warps and 11 wefts per cm.
Warp: 2 ply S, cotton, 0,5 mm, condition 5.
Weft: 2 ply S cotton, 0,5 mm, condition 5.
Red corner tufts: non spun wool condition 3.
Edging yarn : 2 ply S wool 0,5 mm, condition 3.
pH cotton 6,7.

Acquired by:

Collected between 1930-47 by Sven Speyer for the engineering firm Christiani and Nielsen. On exhibit in the firm until 1988 where the textiles of this collection were donated the National Museum.

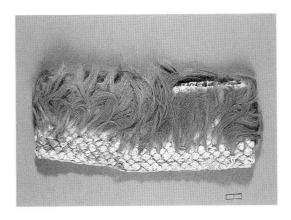

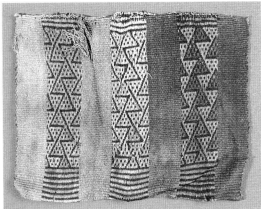

Mus. No.: C.N.8
Type: Cylindrical headband.
Material: Wool.
Technique: Peruke stitch.
Colour: Natural brown foundation with red pile material.
Provenience: Peru.
Size: Cylinder of 56 x 10 cm
Date: Unknown
Cross-reference: none

Description
In this headband the very long, non spun, red pile material is inserted in every single knot. Originally only the first row of knots was without the pile material. The knots are a special form of Peruke stitch – with a double slanting line on one side. The knots measure ca. 12 mm each.

Fibre Analysis
The material is 4 ply S wool, each of 0,8 mm, condition 2.
The loose red wool seems to be top hair fibres and is 8-10 cm long.
pH wool 5,5.

Acquired by:
Collected between 1930-47 by Sven Speyer for the engineering firm Christiani and Nielsen. On exhibit in the firm until 1988, where all the textiles from the collection were donated the National Museum.

Mus. No.: C.N.10
Type: Bag
Material: Supplementary warp pattern
Technique:
Colour: Red, yellow, brown, white
Provenience: Unknown
Size: 18 x 23 cm
Date: 1000 - 1450 AD
Cross-reference: O.4193

Description
Small bag woven in stripes of plain weave warp rep and supplementary warp patterning. Characteristically for this technique the warp patterning starts out with a small piece of plain weave – where the different coloured sheds alternate and make horizontal stripes. Here one shed is brown, and the other shed is red/white or yellow/white.

The bag is complete with 4 selvages.

Fibre Analysis
The weaving has 24 warps and 5 wefts per cm.
Warp: 2 ply S, wool, 0,4 mm, condition 1.
Weft: 2 ply S, wool, 0,7 mm, condition 1.
pH wool warp 4,3.

Acquired by:
Collected between 1930-47 by Sven Speyer for the engineering firm Christiani and Nielsen. On exhibit in the firm until 1988 where the textiles of this collection were donated the National Museum.

Mus. No.: C.N.11
Type: Four-pointed-hat.
Material: Cotton net with wool pile, and knotted wool points.
Technique: Square knot net and "simili velour".
Colour: Non dyed light brown foundation, woollen pile in black, dark and light blue, brown, red, yellow, white.
Provenience: The coast of Peru, (Wari).
Size: Top square 7,5 x 7,5 cm. Cylinder 48,5 x 7,5 cm. Triangle points 2,2 cm at the bottom
Date: 0 – 600 AD
Cross-reference: O.10277

Description

Multi-coloured hat with four pointed corners. The hat is made in a compact net of square knots (top and points) and "simili velour" along the sides. The knots on top are reversed in every other row, to achieve a twill effect, and shaped to close the hat along four diagonal lines from the points to the top of the hat. The four points are knotted in blue wool. The "simili velour" is also a compact net of square knots, but this time with all the knots in the same direction. In every other row coloured woollen yarns are fastened, by letting the wool follow through the square knots along with the cotton foundation yarn. Afterwards the woollen loops are cut so that the final product resembles a Persian rug. The cylinder and the top are knotted vertically, the points horizontally. The knots measure 2 mm each. The woollen knots at the points are slightly smaller.

Fibre Analysis

Floss: 2 ply Z, wool, 0,5 mm, condition 1.
Net: 2 ply S, wool and cotton, 0,4 mm, condition 3.
pH cotton 4,3.

Acquired by:

Collected between 1930-47 by Sven Speyer, for the engineering firm Christiani and Nielsen. On exhibit in the firm until 1988 where the textiles of the collection were donated the National Museum.

Mus. No.: C.N.12
Type: Four-pointed-hat
Material: Wool
Technique: Supplementary warp patterning.
Colour: White/blue/curry/cream/ lavender/-brown
Provenience: Nasca (Wari)
Size: 44 cm around, 7 cm height, top square: 9 x 8 cm
Date: 0 – 600AD
Technical Explanation: Supplementary warp, furred cord "simili velour" technique
Cross-reference: O.4193, C.N.11

Description
The 44 cm (warp) by 8 cm (weft) fabric is sewn together to form a cylinder and the top square is sewn to the top of the cylinder in the middle leaving a 1 cm wide fold of the cylinder fabric in each corner. In these corner folds are placed a furred cord of 1 cm. This cord is made by a net of square knots around a centre cord with extra woollen threads knotted in – "simili velour" technique.

Fibre Analysis
The fabric has 28 warps and 8 wefts per cm.
Warp: 2 ply S wool 0,5 mm, condition 5.
Weft: 2 ply S wool 0,4 mm, condition 3.
Tassels: 2 ply S wool 0,6 mm, condition 2.
Edging yarn: 2 ply S wool 0,5 mm, condition 3.
pH red wool 5,6.

Acquired by:
Collected between 1930–47 by Sven Speyer for the engineering firm Christiani and Nielsen. On exhibit in the firm until 1988 where the textiles of this collection were donated the National Museum.

Mus. No.: C.N.0
Type: Woman's mantle
Material: Wool
Technique: Tapestry and complementary weft weave with substituting colours
Colour: Blue, red, green, yellow, white
Provenience: Chuquibamba
Size: 110 x 120 cm
Date: 1400 - 1550 AD
Cross-reference: O.4261, O.41886

Description

This textile is a women's shawl woven in the Chuquibamba (mountains north of Arequipa) style. It was woven on a vertical frame loom, and would have been the top right quarter of the weaving as it sat on the loom – recognised by the weft selvage with a few thicker warps to reinforce the textile preventing it from getting narrower during weaving, and the top warp selvage recognised by the darned in warp-ends of the terminal selvage (the initial selvage would have warp loops).

The textile has the bottom 13 cm reverse side up (there is a back and a front on the complementary weft weaving) – this is because the textile was worn folded almost in half around the shoulders and fastened with a pin, and so only the right side would be seen, even on the visible lower edge of the inner part of the mantle.

The patterning consists of tapestry woven stars (or flowers) and in between them squares woven in complementary weft weave with substituting

colours. Each of these squares have two alternating wefts creating the pattern (red and blue) and after the weaving white, yellow and green has been embroidered on.

Between the patterns are weft rep stripes. A 10 cm tapestry woven stripe with jaguars cross the fabric horizontally.

Fibre Analysis
There are 8 warps and 28 wefts per cm.
The warp is 2 ply S wool, 0,6 mm, condition 5.
The weft is 2 ply S wool, 0,4 mm, condition 5.
The edge warp is 5 strands of the general weft.
pH warp wool 3,5.
pH weft wool 5,0.

Acquired by:
Collected between 1930 and 1947 by Sven Speyer for the engineering firm Christiani and Nielsen. On exhibit in this firm until 1988 where the textiles of this collection were donated the National Museum.

Mus. No.: U.N.1
Type: Mantle fringe
Material: Wool and cotton
Technique: Loop stitch
Colour: Red, yellow
Provenience: Paracas/Nazca
Size: 25 x 6 cm
Date: ca 200 – 600 AD
Cross-reference: O.6345

Description
As lengthwise core in the fringe is used 6 cotton yarns each one twisted (Z) of two from a doubled 2 ply S twisted yarn. Around this core 4 rows of loop stitches are sewn. The short flaps at an angle from this are sewn with the same technique but without core. The yarn used for the sewing is 2 ply S wool. The looped fringe has along the end of the little flaps been sewn to something – probably a mantle or another fabric.

Fibre Analysis
The woollen yarn consists of fibres between 0.02-0.03 mm. The fibres are loosely spun and loosely twisted at a 30 angle. The thickness of the twisted threads is 1 mm.
Wool, 2 ply S, 0,4 mm, condition 3.
pH wool 3,5.
pH inner cotton 6,4.

Acquired by:
Unknown.